NO
BIGGER
THAN
NECESSARY

NO BIGGER THAN NECESSARY

AN ALTERNATIVE TO SOCIALISM, CAPITALISM, AND ANARCHISM

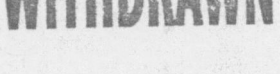

Andrew M. Greeley

A MERIDIAN BOOK
NEW AMERICAN LIBRARY
TIMES MIRROR
NEW YORK AND SCARBOROUGH, ONTARIO
THE NEW ENGLISH LIBRARY LIMITED, LONDON

PERMISSIONS ACKNOWLEDGMENTS

Quotations from Reinhold Niebuhr: Reprinted by permission of
Charles Scribner's Sons from THE NATURE AND DESTINY OF
MAN, *Volume One, Human Nature*, by Reinhold Niebuhr. Copyright
1941 by Charles Scribner's Sons.
Quotations from Daniel Bell: From THE CULTURAL
CONTRADICTIONS OF CAPITALISM by Daniel Bell. Copyright
© 1976 by Daniel Bell. Basic Books, Inc., Publishers, New York.

First Meridian Printing, October, 1977

1 2 3 4 5 6 7 8 9

PRINTED IN THE UNITED STATES OF AMERICA

To Geno Baroni

Acknowledgments

That this exercise is not more awkward is the result of many useful comments and suggestions I received from such people as Ralph Whitehead, Basil Whiting, William McCready, Pastora San Juan Cafferty, Zdzislawa Walaczek, James Coleman, Terry Clark, Arthur Stinchcombe, David Greenstone, David Tracy. I will absolve them (with all appropriate plenary indulgences) from whatever furies this book may unleash; however, I warn them that I will expect them to be on my side of the bar when the lights go back on.

I am grateful to Walter Carringer, chairman of the Mars Lecture Committee, Northwestern University, to Raymond Mack, provost of Northwestern, Professor David Epperson of the education department, and to John Matthias Krump, Catholic chaplain at Northwestern, for the courtesy shown me during my three evenings in Wildcat land.

Contents

CHAPTER 1

ॐ ॐ ॐ

Picture, Model,
Theory, and Ethic

THIS book began with my re-
flections upon the apparent proclivity of "white ethnics" to
respond differently than other groups in American society to
certain social and social-policy situations. To be more precise
and more personal, it arose from my sense of general mystifica-
tion over the obvious fact that I tend to look at society in a
rather different fashion than many of my colleagues.

Thus my colleague and friend James S. Coleman opens his
book, *Power and the Structure of Society*, with the sentence,
"The common-sense way of viewing society is as a vast network or organization of persons." I would immediately add
the words "and groups" to Coleman's introductory sentence. I
would also want to make it much clearer in the course of the
book that the "corporate actors" with which he is concerned
are in fact "corporate networks." Every other sentence in the
book I find insightful, helpful, and agreeable; and our interests
recently have converged remarkably. But I wonder why I
want to throw a reference to "networks" and "groups" into
his view of society. Or to ask it the other way, since I know
Coleman does not deny the importance of groups and networks in society, why does he feel it acceptable to leave them

implicit in his first sentence and I find it imperative to insist that a reference to them be explicit as a statement of the first premise.

Simultaneously I reflected on the fact that our principal benefactor, the Ford Foundation, was in the process of choosing a leader. Gurus and wise men from all over were solicited to write position papers. Some of them will go into a week-long retreat with the trustees of the foundation; after it, the trustees will produce a lengthy job description of the man who will succeed Mr. Bundy, and they will begin the long search for someone who fits the job description. I almost wrote, "a long search for the man they wanted to give the job to anyhow." And I almost wrote that not to accuse the trustees of the Ford Foundation of conspiracy but rather to suggest that it is certainly the way I would have proceeded, and I would surely not hold it against them if they went through the long formal process (I do not say "charade") to legitimate the choice. Why not? Because you find the man who's good for the job and then you look up reasons for hiring him.

In the "Ford Selection Procedure" the process is not merely a rationalization; it is something that *ought* to be done, and one really *ought* to suspend judgment until the process is finished. After all, if one acts on the basis of instinct, impulse, "feel," intuition, one might make a mistake. Yet I note that one might just as well make a mistake if one permits the rational, universalist search process to destroy the ingenuity, spontaneity, and brilliance of the original intuitive and instinctive insight.

One could argue the issue forever, and it is not my purpose in this book to do so. I am intrigued, rather, by the fact of the difference and by the increasing social-science evidence that such differences in style of social behavior are not merely widespread in American society but also apparently correlate at a moderately high level with religion. Maybe Max Weber was right about the Protestant ethic but wrong in thinking that its primary impact was economic.

In trying to cope with the phenomenon of what I will term the "Catholic ethic" I found myself rediscovering the old "Catholic social theory" in which I was raised during my seminary years. I discovered to my surprise that the theory was alive and well (though without the Catholic name) in such interesting places as the economic thinking of the Overseas Development Council and in E. F. Schumacher's book, *Small Is Beautiful*.[1] Sometime after the Second Vatican Council, most American Catholics with social concerns abandoned this theory; they are presently talking about "Marxism" and "Liberation Theology." (If you're Number 2, you have to try harder, I suppose.) And while they are busy with their new concerns, something rather like what the Catholic Rural Life Council*' was preaching back in the 1930s and 1940s, and also something rather like what Emmanuel Mounier, Jacques Maritain, Eric Gill, and Hilaire Belloc were articulating, is now being pushed by an increasing number of international economists as the solution to the world's food problem.†

What began as a search for a sociological explanation has developed into an explicit conviction (though I suspect that I have held it implicitly all along) that the issue of capitalism or socialism is a false dichotomy (even granting that there are many different kinds of both). There are other political ideologies that provide other—and many, I would argue, far more humane—approaches to the problem of man and society.‡

My primary premise is that humans approach society with a collection of "pictures" tucked away in the back of their heads. They use these pictures to organize and interpret the multidinous phenomena that impinge on their consciousness. These pictures, "templates," or "road maps" organize and de-

---

* The National Catholic Rural Life Council is a Catholic organization that tries to apply Catholic social theory to farming and in particular to farm family life. It was insistent in the 1930s and '40s on the importance of the single-family farm. Emmanuel Mounier was a French Catholic philosopher who developed an elaborate theory of Christian personalism with strong social-action implications. Jacques Maritain was a Catholic neothomist philosopher who developed within a thomistic context a theory of pluralism and democracy. Eric Gill, an English Catholic artist, and Hilaire Belloc, an English Catholic writer, espoused "distributism," a political theory which advocated the dismantling of large corporate structures of the capitalist society.

† It is another case of Greeley's Law: When Catholics Stop Something, Everybody Else Starts It. This is actually Greeley's Second Law. The first is, When Everybody Stops Something, Catholics Start It.

‡ Please note that I do not use the word "ideology" in a pejorative sense.

fine experience and prescribe the more or less spontaneous common-sense response to situations. At a more formal level, they are what anthropologist Clifford Geertz calls "meaning systems." The pictures are the symbols that constitute the various levels of meaning system: religion, common sense, science, history, and so forth.

Sociologist David Matza describes how these pictures work:

> Since assumptions are usually implicit, they tend to remain beyond the reach of such intellectual correctives as argument, criticism, and scrutiny. Thus, to render assumptions explicit is not only to propose a thesis; more fundamentally it is to widen and deepen the area requiring exploration. Assumptions implicit in conceptions are rarely inconsequential. Left unattended, they return to haunt us by shaping or bending theories that purport to explain major social phenomena. Assumptions may prompt us to notice or to ignore discrepancies or patterns that may be observed in the empirical world. Conceptions structure our inquiry.[2]

I'm not altogether sure where these pictures come from, though I would agree with Matza that they are both implicit and normative; they are assumptions about the way things are and the way things should be, and they are generally held antecedent to any self-conscious reflection. It is difficult to argue about such pictures because one must first persuade the other that he even has a picture that is different from that which could be held by any other reasonable person. Those who have different pictures, as I have discovered in my dialogue with Orlando Patterson, professor of sociology at Harvard, must be inferior and quite possibly immoral not to view the world in the same way that "all sensible" people do. Arguments about pictures very quickly turn into moral denunciation. I think one cannot even begin to be a sensitive and objective thinker until one becomes conscious of one's own pictures.

At that point the pictures become models. They lose some of their color and vividness and power to generate spontaneous response when we make them self-conscious. A model rarely leads us to poke someone in the mouth for being an irrational sonofabitch, and hence, when pictures become models, dialogue can become more civil and social interaction less violent. However, the model does lack the power, vitality, spontaneity, and the creativity of the implicit picture.

There will be a good deal of talk about models in this book, so I digress for a moment of epistemology. Until I read Ian Barbour's book on models, *Myths, Models, and Paradigms*,[3] I was happily content with saying that models were nothing more than tools for viewing reality and that the issue was not whether a model was true or false, but whether it was a useful tool or not. (In this I followed Max Weber.) However, I am now persuaded that such nominalism does not go far enough; I agree with Barbour that the model is also a tentative working description of reality, in addition to being an abstraction from it. It does not claim to be a complete description of reality but rather a useful tool that tentatively sketches out in broad, oversimplified strokes the outline of reality. Surely it is the case that with the models I am concerned with in this book— models that arise from our basic pictures of reality—the model is more than a tool, since it is, I contend, a self-conscious abstraction from the picture (or the symbol) that guides our interpretation of and our response to the phenomena of daily experience.

A "theory," in the sense the word is used in this book, is an integrated system of models—that is to say, a self-conscious, explicit, and abstract, formally integrated system of pictures in the back of our heads, or, to use a term that may be more precise than "back of our heads," the pictures reside in our "preconscious." Our various pictures are connected loosely, unselfconsciously, and with links that are as much psychological as logical. When we make these symbols self-conscious, explicit, and abstract, and link them together in a unity that is at least partially artificial, we have a "theory" that is in itself a model but now one derived not from an individual symbol, but from a whole symbol system.

When the theory becomes more than descriptive (and theories very quickly do) and becomes a norm for decision-making and for the eventual elaboration of social policy, then I would submit that the theory becomes an "ethic." When one combines two or more ethical dimensions and invests this combination with strong personal emotional commitment, one has what I will call an explicit "ideology."

Most people, however, are not explicit ideologues. Their responses to social situations result not so much from checking with tables that lay out their ideological system as from the resonances that a situation stirs up among the intersecting vectors and dynamisms of the pictures (or symbols) that the person is toting around in his preconscious. (It hardly needs to be said that the pictures or symbols are dynamic; they do not merely "apprehend" reality, they also interpret it, resonate to it, actually construct it.)

I will suggest in this book that there is a social ideology based on the traditional teaching of the Catholic Church that differs fundamentally from the other three major ideologies that I observe in the contemporary Western world: socialism, capitalism, and anarchism. This ideology, I will suggest, tends to be found (though not exclusively and not totally) in the preconscious of Catholics. It is articulated formally and self-consciously in the Catholic social theory to be found in the papal encyclicals and the writings of such Catholic theorists as Jacques Maritain, Yves Simon, and Emmanuel Mounier, and, I would hasten to add, in the daily activities of many practicing Catholics who are politicians, union leaders, community organizers, or even parish priests.

Where did these pictures come from and where do they "exist"? I am sure that they are *not* in clearly defined categories, as Noam Chomsky's rules of grammar (or "deep syntax") seem to be, yet they are powerfully rooted in our personalities, leading me to suspect that they are acquired very early in the socialization experience—perhaps at about the same time and maybe even as part of the process of developing sexual identity and religious world view.[4] While the issue is beyond the scope of our discussion here, it seems likely to me that one's ideological symbol system (unselfconscious ideology) is put together from a set of pictures one absorbs by watching one's mother and father respond to the social reality that they experience; one absorbs these pictures very early in the game.

I must defer to psychologists and the physiologists of perception on the issue of what physically and metaphysically these pictures are; in truth I am not even sure what physically and metaphysically the preconscious is (though systems as different as Thomism and psychoanalysis are both led to postulate it—the Thomists calling it the "agent intellect"). If someone tells me that a set of interconnected pictures may constitute a gestalt, I'm perfectly prepared to agree with such a comment, again leaving to the psychologists, the physiologists, and the metaphysicians the issue of what is a gestalt. I can only appeal to the reader to examine his own experience to determine whether he has such interconnected systems of pictures with which he resonates to reality.

But if we obtain our symbol systems largely from our parents, the question then arises, whence do they obtain them? To push matters back to the beginning, if there are somewhat different symbol systems or "ethics" to be found in Protestants than Catholics, how come?

As will be noted in the next chapter, David Tracy* has outlined fundamentally different "styles of religious reflection" in the Catholic and in the Protestant theological traditions, styles which, perhaps not surprisingly, correspond rather neatly with the social and political ideologies of the two denominational traditions. My response to the question of leadership selection, for example, can easily be subsumed under an "analogic" world view, and my colleagues from Protestant backgrounds can subsume theirs under a "dialectical" world view, to use Father Tracy's vocabulary. But where did these differences in style of religious reflection come from in the first place? And what is the nature of the relationship between the formal "high-level" tradition of religious reflection and the day-to-day ideological responses of Protestants and Catholics to social problems and to social-policy questions?

Do the different styles of religious reflection in fact reflect an even more basic difference in cosmology and theology in the strictest sense of the words? Is the Catholic ideology ultimately rooted in a somewhat more benign view of the uni-

* Professor David Tracy, Divinity School, University of Chicago. His book, *The Analogical Imagination*, will be published by Seabury Press, 1978.

verse and in the ultimate power that underpins the universe? Is the Catholic God an "ethnic?" Might He even be a precinct captain?

The issue is a fascinating one, it goes far below the scope of the present essay—quite possibly beyond the present capacity of anyone to offer a response. (I eagerly await Father Tracy's book on the subject.) I cannot resist the temptation to point out that an ethnic, precinct-captain God does correspond rather nicely to Alfred North Whitehead's process theology notion of God as the Great Improviser.

Similarly, I would like to note the distinction between the "high" tradition and the "low" tradition principally to indicate that far more study is required on the subject before any confident delineations can be advanced. Did Philip Murray organize the United Steelworkers of America and then administer the Congress of Industrial Organization the way he did because he had read the papal social encyclicals? Murray delighted in the social encyclicals, studied them carefully, and quoted them at great length whenever the occasion arose—and particularly when the occasion was before a mostly Catholic audience. But one can hardly escape the conclusion that Murray rejoiced in the encyclicals not because they shaped his thinking, or even because they confirmed it, but rather because they agreed with it. Similarly, James Edward Quigley, the genius whose pluralistic solution kept the Archdiocese of Chicago together during the crisis of the 1900–1914 immigration, respected the freedom and independence of the Poles, the Slovaks, the Lithuanians, the Croats, Slovenes, and all the other migrants to his "Hapsburg Empire" in miniature not because he had read about social pluralism in the encyclical *Rerum novarum* but because he was the canny descendant of the Famine Irish, who had absorbed the political skills of pluralism about the same time he learned to talk.[5]

Truly there is a dialogue going on between the high tradition and the low, but until much more historical and psychological research is available, I shall provisionally conclude that the high tradition is an articulation, a formalization, a reassertion, and a validation of the low tradition far more than it is a cause.

I argue that the "high" Catholic social theory is in fact a reflection of a fundamental Catholic viewpoint on the nature of human nature and the nature of human society that affects perspectives and behavior of ordinary Catholics. The "high" tradition articulates and formalizes the "low" tradition and reinforces and validates it.

The remote origins of the high Catholic social-theory tradition can be found in the work of the medieval theologians both as they reinterpreted the Aristotelian views of the nature of human society and as they sought for a definition of the state to clarify the issues in the Church-state controversies of the late Middle Ages. However, the articulation of a formal Catholic social theory by the Church began only in 1891 with the publication of Pope Leo XIII's encyclical *Rerum novarum* (*On the Condition of the Working Classes*). This encyclical in its turn was the result of the intellectual ferment of the nineteenth century, beginning with the Catholic reaction to the French Revolution in the works of Lacordaire and de Lamennais (a reaction in the liberal direction) and Chateaubriand (in the conservative direction). At the same time, Catholic involvement, in coping with the problems that the Industrial Revolution was creating for the working class, produced men such as Frédéric Ozanam, who founded the Society of St. Vincent de Paul to aid the poor; Montalembert, who as a member of the French Chamber of Deputies wrote the first factory legislation in France; and the Catholic "workers' circles," organized in France by Albert de Mun and La Tour du Pin. At the same time, in Germany, the worker-turned-priest Adolph Kolping, the government bureaucrat-turned-bishop Emmanuel von Ketteler, and the charming and fascinating hunchback politician Ludwig Windhorst denounced the oppressions of capitalism on the working class with at least as much vigor if not as much long-term impact as Marx.

A full intellectual history of how the mystic theologians, romantic philosophers, and practical activists set up the ferment that led to *Rerum novarum* has yet to be written. However, it seems safe to say that there was a good deal more input from non-Catholic social criticism than *Rerum novarum* explicitly admits. (We know, to cite a twentieth-century example, that labor priest John A. Ryan was strongly influenced by the non-Catholic populist tradition of his native Minnesota.)

Rerum novarum was essentially a defense of the rights of the working man combined with a vigorous condemnation of nineteenth-century socialism. Forty years after the encyclical *Quadragesimo anno* came closer to articulating a positive Catholic view of an organic society in particular by laying out the three cardinal principles of Catholic social theory: *personalism, subsidiarity*, and *pluralism. Personalism* insists that the goal of the society is to develop and enrich the individual human person; the state and society exist for the person and not vice versa. *Subsidiarity* insists that no organization should be bigger than necessary and that nothing should be done by a large and higher social unit than can be done effectively by a lower and smaller unit. *Pluralism* contends that a healthy society is characterized by a wide variety of intermediate groups freely flourishing between the individual and the state.

In the wake of *Quadragesimo anno* there was a flowering of Catholic social-action movements in the United States. In the 1930s and 1940s there were Catholic labor schools, the Association of Catholic Trade Unionists, and in Chicago, the Catholic Council on Working Life. There were also groups such as the Catholic Interracial Council and the Catholic Conference on Religion and Race, the National Catholic Rural Life Conference—each of which tried to articulate concrete social policies that were derived from the theoretical perspectives laid down in *Quadragesimo anno*. In addition, activist groups such as the Young Christian Workers and the Young Students and the Christian Family Movement enjoyed considerable vigor in the years between the end of World War II and the Second Vatican Council. Of all these organizations, only the Christian Family Movement enjoyed substantial vitality in the wake of the postconciliar reaction and disillusionment.

In other countries there were parallel developments. In England the Distributus political movement of Chesterton and Belloc, and later Eric Gill, claimed to articulate a traditional Catholic social perspective. In France the philosophical writings of Jacques Maritain and Emmanuel Mounier and the organizational activity of Canon (later Cardinal) Cardijn pro-

duced a remarkable flowering of Catholic social teaching and
activity after the 1945 liberation. The Christian democratic
parties of Europe (like the corporatist party of Dollfuss and
Scheussnig in Austria and, with less justification, the one-party
government of Spain and Portugal) claimed to be inspired by
the Catholic social theory, as laid down in the encyclicals, and
were often staffed in their earliest years by the militants
trained in Canon Cardijn's Young Christian Worker and
Young Christian Student movements or by products of the
western European Catholic trade-union federations.

Unfortunately, the Christian democratic parties have apparently not been able to articulate social programs that differ,
save in detail, from the programs of the social democratic
parties. The CDU in Germany thus may be a "conservative"
alternative to the SPD "socialist" party, but surely the differences between the two are mostly of degree and not of kind.
This book is not the place to analyze the success and the failures of the Christian democratic parties, but it has been suggested to me by some European theorists that in the final
analysis the parties failed because they did not take seriously
enough the principle of subsidiarity laid down by *Quadragesimo anno*. They became centralizing bureaucracies, working within the constraints of the centralizing bureaucratic
state. The Christian democratic parties, in other words, were
not nearly so "radical" as they should be, considering that they
were theoretically decentralizers and localists. In the intellectual climate of Europe between 1945 and 1965, it might well
have been impossible seriously to think that a localist and
decentralizing position would have any political success.

Despite the immense encyclical output of Pius XII, it was
only with the advent of John XXIII in the 1960s that major
new social documents emerged from Rome. In *Mater et magistra* and *Pacem in terris*, Pope John brought to brilliant fruition
the theorizing of the previous seven decades. *Mater et magistra*
updated *Quadragesimo anno* and laid out a strong, positive
defense of the integrity of the human person and the social
rights and obligations of that person in the modern world.
Much less than his predecessors was John disturbed by the
world he saw around him, and much more than any pope in

recent memory was he capable of seeing the opportunity in the human quest for freedom, justice, and dignity, and the contributions the Catholic tradition could make to that quest. In *Pacem in terris* he turned to the world economic and political order and, in what may be the most successful of all papal encyclicals, applied to world problems the Catholic social-theoretical perspective.

Paul VI's encyclical *Populorum progressio* may mark the decisive shift away from the distinctively Catholic social theory to watered-down Marxism. Previous papal social encyclicals were solidly in the Catholic tradition, but *Populorum progressio* was substantially the work of the French Marxist Lebret, whose passionate hatred for the United States was only barely concealed by the subsequent editing by Roman authorities. No one, as far as I am aware, has noted the massive shift of emphasis between *Quadragesimo anno* and *Pacem in terris*, on the one hand, and *Populorum progressio*, on the other. It may well be that Paul VI's social encyclical will have had as disastrous an effect on the Catholic social ethic as *Humanae vitae* did on the Catholic sexual ethic.

In the United States, two movements seem to have combined to replace the old social action and social theory with a new and romantic soft-core socialism: the importation of liberation theology and Paulo Freire's consciousness-raising from Latin America and the "liturgical protest" style of the Berrigans. In discussion with those influenced by both these phenomena it is useless to argue that liberation theology has had little impact on Latin America and that the Berrigan style was counterproductive for the peace movement. Berrigan and Freire are beyond challenge. What is baffling to me is the absolute silence of the bearers of the older Catholic social tradition in the face of these twin assaults, as well as their apparent lack of awareness that there are now a substantial number of non-Catholics who are embracing those social principles and perspectives that they are apparently not prepared to defend.

We may well have seen the end of "encyclical social theory." The papacy at the present time does not have the prestige to command a very large audience even within the Church for further social documents; it is unlikely to recapture such an audience unless it comes to terms honestly with the world population crisis. But even if a new, more popular, and more credible pope should appear on the scene, it does not seem likely that he could do better than elaborate on the triple principle of personalism, pluralism, and subsidiarity. Further contributions of theory are much more likely to come from those who try to implement these three subprinciples in restructuring Catholic social theory and from those who have practiced the three principles (perhaps without realizing it) in their own social and political careers. (At least 70 percent of what Governor Jerry Brown said in his interview with *Playboy* magazine, for example, was a rearticulation of the Catholic social theory filtered through his experience as governor of California at a time when localism and decentralization are just being rediscovered. It would be absurd to say that theologically Jerry Brown has more authority to speak on social matters than the pope, but existentially, Brown doubtless now has a much wider audience in the United States.)

Intellectual development cannot be forced. The development of antisocial thought takes time, effort, and experience. If a rediscovery of a Catholic social ethic does animate the careers of men and women in the years ahead, seeking subsidiarity, pluralism, and personalism in human life, then at some later point the experiences of these men and women may be formalized in yet another Roman document—if not an encyclical, then perhaps a statement from a general council or from an international council of bishops.*

I must say a word about the use of the term "Catholic" in this book. To say that the ideology with which this book is principally concerned is Catholic is not to contend that Catholicism has a monopoly on the ideology or that the Catholic Church as a human institution or Catholics as individuals have

---

*The classic statement available in English of the Catholic social theory is to be found in Johannes A. Messner, *Social Ethics: Natural Law in the Modern World* (St. Louis: B. Herder Book Co., 1949), a translation from German of a volume written over thirty years ago. More recently, Harvard professor Roberto Unger has begun to publish an updated and American version of the Catholic social theory without any explicit reference to its Catholic origins, *Law in Modern Society: Toward a Criticism of Social Theory* (New York: The Free Press, 1976).

always practiced it. No institution or individual ever lives up even to the approximation of its ideals, and no ideology is so unique and so special that it does not share many, or most, or even all of its models with individuals and groups from other traditions and heritages.

Thus the ideology I describe in subsequent chapters has very much in common with Buddhist ideology as E. F. Schumacher describes it; it also agrees in many respects (though I think not all) with the anarchism of Proudhon, and in some respects with the more modern anarchism of Theodore Roszak (who, after all, started out as a Catholic). Similarly, the Catholic ideology that I shall describe has substantially more in common with the social and political world view of Thomas Jefferson and the other Founding Fathers than those worthies did, it seems to me, with liberal capitalism's utilitarian ethic, which became more or less official in the United States from, let us say, 1850 to 1950.

And, of course, the Catholic Church has not always practiced what it preached—to put the matter modestly. An organization that in the course of its history has made alliance with tyrants, sold out to establishments, violated human consciences, forced conversions, presided over the Inquisition, and repressed the pluralism of Matteo Ricci in China and Roberto di Nobile in India (men who wanted to develop an authentic "Indian" and "Chinese" Catholicism), hardly offers a shining example of what I call in this book the Catholic ethic. To bring the matter into more recent context, it would be absurd to suggest that the current papacy practices the principle of subsidiarity that it so fervently preaches.* It was said in our seminary days that the Catholic Church is the first to talk about a living wage and the last to pay it. That accusation may not be altogether outmoded even today. It is also surely true that the Catholic Church frequently is the first to talk about decentralization and the last to actually decentralize its own power.

Nevertheless, such indictments overlook some important

---

* Actually, subsidiarity began to wane in the Church when the cable and the steamship reinforced the autocratic propensities of the Renaissance papacy.

data: of all the multinational organizations in the world, the first one may still be on balance the most decentralized. A bishop probably has more power in his diocese than a regional manager does in a multinational corporation, and a pastor certainly has more power in a parish than a plant manager or a store manager would in a multinational corporation. ("Every bishop a pope in his own diocese, every pastor a bishop in his own parish." There is a good deal of truth in the ironic slogan.) Sometimes the reasons for decentralization are neglect and incompetence. Yet to some considerable extent at least, the Catholic Church as a human institution, for all its imperfections, does give some hint in its organizational structure and style that the people who belong to it may be a little bit more disposed to grass-roots decision-making than are other human institutions.

However, the past or the present virtues of the Roman Church are not the issue; if one is interested in understanding why ethnics have different unselfconscious political and social ideologies, the accurate and precise answer, it seems to me, is "because they are Catholics."

It would be an interesting subject for historical research to trace the links between the Jeffersonian vision of society, for example, and that of Philip Murray or James E. Quigley. Do both reflect in some sense a world view that is not only pre-industrial and pre-Lutheran but even pre-Roman? And does the similarity between the Buddhist ideology and the Catholic suggest that what we are dealing with is in fact an archaic ethic, one that goes back very far into the past and down very deep into the human unconscious. Buddhism began in India, and the similarity in laws between the ancient Celts and the ancient Indians indicate an intimate link between the two societies in their Indo-European matrix. At least such a possibility deserves exploration.

Call it what you want, the "communal ethic" (a phrase I have lifted from Ralph Whitehead of the University of Massachusetts), or the "neighborhood ethic" (the phrase of my colleague William McCready), or the "Catholic ethic." The point of this volume is that there is a systematic, well-integrated, ideological system that makes a vigorous claim—and to many

also an attractive claim—to be an alternative to the false dilemma of capitalism or socialism.

To those non-Catholics who are interested in understanding
why Catholics have a special approach to social-policy questions, the book may be a useful explanation of the ideology
that comes out of the Catholic heritage. To those few Catholics who still think there is an unique or special contribution
that their heritage can make to the current conversation, this
book might also serve as a stimulus to think through again or
to think about for the first time what illumination the Catholic
political and social tradition might shed on present human
ambiguities and dilemmas.

In pursuing my primary purpose—outlining a Catholic social ethic and pointing at certain policy implications of such an
ethic—I shall make use of the ideas and the writings of many
other authors. If I were German, I would quote these authors
at great length, not being content with a few words or phrases
on a paradigm and an occasional quick summary paragraph.
The result would be a massive *wissenschaftlich* volume which
would be prohibitively expensive and in which the main
themes of my reconnaissance would in all likelihood get lost.
Nor would I in that case still be fair to the nuances, the qualifi-
cations, the refinements of the thought of those whom I cite or
on whom I rely. The only fair way to state the thought of
another is to give it in its entirety. Anyone who wishes to
understand adequately the thought of Geertz, Arendt, or
Roszak should read their books, in addition to mine. Doubtless,
I will oversimplify their positions, but all writing is oversimpli-
fication. The pertinent question is not whether an author
oversimplifies but whether his simplifications are in keeping
with his purposes. Similarly, though I hope I am not unfair to
the other three ideologies that I describe in this book, my
principal purpose is to sketch out what I take to be the Catholic (or "communal" or "archaic" or "neighborhood") ideology. Anyone who wants to know what capitalism or socialism
or anarchism stands for in all the rich nuances of its details
can consult books sympathetic to such positions. My purpose
in this volume is not to argue with the capitalists, socialists, or
anarchists, but rather to delineate how I think the Catholic

ideology differs from theirs—especially since I think that in the final analysis argument about such ideological differences is largely fruitless. What one contributes to the discussion, it seems to me, is not a refutation of the other position but rather a statement of what contributions one's own particular heritage may make to an improvement of the human condition. As a broad outline, I will contend that my paradigm is not basically unfair to the other three ideologies, and I would submit that that is the only requirement that can be imposed on a book with the very specific purposes the present volume has. (And I also presume that the reader will concede me the right to work my purposes and not what might be his.)

I trust that this introduction, as it sidesteps cautiously through inadequate data, nonexistent research, ambiguous terminology, and uncertain assumptions, will be sufficient evidence to the reader that the present volume is an exercise in thinking out loud; it is a first tentative peek, an attempt to raise, awkwardly and clumsily perhaps, some fundamental and important issues that some people may want to discuss further.

Because of the exploratory nature of this book I have kept the tone informal, if only to remind the reader periodically that I am attempting to begin a discussion and not end one.

CHAPTER 2

ᖃ ᖃ ᖃ

Ideologies
and Styles

IDEOLOGY, Clifford Geertz
has rightly observed, is a term with a bad reputation in social
science, mostly because the people who originally wrote about
it were principally concerned with the narrow and rigid totalitarian ideologies of the left or the right that plagued Europe
until 1950, when the right-wing ideologies disappeared (with
the exception of Spain and Portugal) from power, leaving the
left-wing ideologies opportunities to deliver on their promises,
which they generally failed to do. But in the context of commentary on ideology between the two world wars, most authors
were concerned about German Nazism, Russian communism,
and Italian fascism. In such a context, ideology came to mean a
rigid, all-demanding, and all-controlling intellectual system that
interpreted every aspect of reality and demanded complete and
unconditional assent to all of its interpretations and programs.
Ideology was not merely a political and social perspective; it
was a quasi-faith, a pseudoreligion, and in the postwar writing
of authors such as Edward Shils, this dark, foreboding aspect
of ideology continued to be emphasized. McCarthyism was
pointed to in horror as an emerging American ideology, though
historically the comparison of McCarthy (surely no prize) with

Hitler or Stalin looks almost as paranoid as the late senator was himself. Later, such authors as Daniel Bell and Seymour Lipset hailed "the end of ideology," by which they seemed to be suggesting that social and political policies would be designed in the future not by those who had rigid and preprogrammed solutions, but by competent, pragmatic technicians. With the resurgence of the left in the 1960s and the imitation of the rigid, doctrinaire approach of a handful of blacks and perhaps a larger number of feminists in the early 1970s, it looked like the Bell-Lipset prophecy was in error. Surely both the civil-rights and feminist movements in their worst manifestations imposed an intellectual discipline, a rigid thought control, and a systematic quasi-paranoid interpretation of all phenomena such that its style if not its substance was uncomfortably reminiscent of earlier rigid ideologies. If Bell and Lipset had meant that ideologues were to disappear from the face of the earth, they were clearly wrong. Narrow, rigid personalities are likely to be with us for the foreseeable future. If, however, Bell and Lipset meant that the time was over when ideologues could have any major influence on the course of national policy, they may well have been right.

Geertz suggests, however, that in order that the concept "ideology" might escape from the dilemmas that plague its use, one must redefine the concept, and in his classic essay "Ideology as a Cultural System"[1] Geertz takes most of the negative sting out of the term. Ideology for him is simply a symbol system, a set of templates with high emotional charge and strong moral investment that provides a chart by which a person can find his way through a complex, confused, and disorganized social reality. Thus, according to Geertz, Winston Churchill's classic statement, "We shall fight on the beaches, we shall fight on the landing grounds, we shall fight in the fields . . ." was not a literal statement of policy but a highly dramatic emotional symbol around which the people of England could rally. Geertz notes that after these stirring words Churchill is supposed to have turned to an aide and said in a nonideological but highly realistic comment, "And we shall hit them over the head with soda-water bottles, because we haven't any guns."

In this book I propose to go even further than Geertz in defanging the term "ideology." As I use it, an ideology need not have a strong emotional or moral charge, as it does in Geertz's use; and it need not be a response to a situation of acute social disorganization. Though I would agree that ideologies can have strong emotional and moral investments and that indeed on occasion they do respond to highly disorganized situations, an ideology, as I use the word, is merely a set of assumptions (preconscious symbols or preconscious models) that provide a perspective (though a dynamic and responsive perspective, a set of normative vectors instead of a set of passive receptors) with which one approaches social and political reality. I shall argue in this book that the vectors can be profitably systematized by asking what assumptions a particular viewpoint makes about the nature of human nature and the phenomenon generally labeled "modernization," which is, in effect, a model of the nature of human society. Ideology, in other words, is when the modernization vector intersects with the nature-of-human-nature vector. How much emotional energy and moral fervor you invest in that intersection depends on a wide variety of personal and social circumstances; but the pictures, or symbols, that cluster around the intersection, though they may be deeply rooted in the preconscious, are not necessarily the sorts of things that under normal circumstances would lead one into the streets and behind the barricades. However—and here, I think, is where I go beyond Geertz—the cluster of symbols around the intersection of modernization and human nature are likely to have considerable influence on how you resonate with and respond to ordinary and commonplace social issues.

Why human nature and modernization? One could, of course, come up with other issues, but I would suggest that the tendency, at least in the North Atlantic world today, is to approach all major social and political questions from a joint concern about how far you can trust ordinary people to be cooperative and how intimately you must involve yourself in the inevitable (or highly probable) forward march of progress. Virtually all ideological writers are either implicitly or explicitly concerned with those two fundamental issues. If one takes at random, for example, such different writers as Theodore Roszak, Konrad Lorenz, and Erich Fromm, one sees that they are preoccupied with the goodness or badness of humankind and with the surge forward toward paradise or destruction. It does not occur to such writers to question the pertinence of discussing whether humankind is good or bad, or the utility—to say nothing of the fruitfulness—of evolutionary assumptions. An occasional author such as Robert Nisbet may argue that because you have change, it does not necessarily follow that change is directional either forward or backward. But most ideological writers, true products of the Western world as they are, seem compelled to assume that you do have direction—much of it downward, according to some currently fashionable ideological critics.

Yet both questions do not normally occur in a non-Western context. Indian philosophers, for example, to the extent that they are not influenced by Western thought, are not concerned with progress but rather with repetition, and devote practically no time or energy to questioning the nature of human nature. Most of them assume, it would seem, that human nature is bad, an assumption they would share with virtually all universalist philosophers outside the Jewish tradition who have emerged since the "axial era,"* as Karl Jaspers called it.

Both the issue of progress and the issue of the nature of human nature are Western—indeed, Western Christian—and, to be specific, Augustinian ideas. Nisbet has persuasively demonstrated that the question of evolution, progress, directional change, did not begin with *The Origin of Species* or *Das Kapital*; it began with *The City of God*. Similarly, doubt about whether human nature is good (as the mostly preaxial Jews would have thought) or bad (as the Greek Platonists certainly thought) managed to focus themselves in the passionate, troubled, mystical soul of Augustine as he listened to the debate between the Persian philosopher Manes, on the one hand, and the Celtic monk Pelagius, on the other. The former

---

* A time in the first millennium before the common era when the world religions emerged and there was a notable increase in self-awareness in human reflection.

was convinced of the fundamental evil of all spirit that was so unfortunate as to be incarcerated in the body, and the latter argued for the fundamental goodness of all that God had created. Augustine—at the risk of oversimplifying a complex issue and an intensely painful personal experience—could see a point to both sides. What God had created was good, but as he experienced it in his own soul, the good was badly flawed by sin, a sin that predisposed one to do evil most of the time. Human nature, in the final analysis, would be redeemed from sinfulness by Jesus, but it could not be cured of its sinful ways. Augustine rejected both Manes and Pelagius (the latter far more vigorously) because in practice it seemed to Augustine, the passionate sinner, that Pelagius was far more a threat to the spiritual life than Manes—and he devised his own synthesis, which in various forms and interpretations has been the Christian compromise solution ever since.

We need not detain ourselves with the details of the Augustinian synthesis. The good Bishop of Hippo himself seems to have ended up leaning more in the direction of the Manichaeans than the Pelagians, but as he was reinterpreted by Thomas Aquinas in what has become the official Catholic position, the pendulum swung back in the other direction of the Irish monk. Reinhold Niebuhr, fierce and passionate Augustinian that he was, saw this quite clearly. He dismissed the Catholic social theory as "semi-Pelagian." The Catholic position, Niebuhr argued, was so optimistic about human nature as to depart the bonds of Christian orthodoxy (by which he meant Augustinian orthodoxy) and become heretical. Paradoxically enough, we shall see in the next chapter that the shift toward pessimism that has occurred since Niebuhr has become so dramatic and so powerful that today many would think that the "liberal" Niebuhr himself is far too optimistic about human nature. Compared to Robert Heilbroner, for example, Niebuhr becomes semi-Pelagian himself.

So the issue was temporarily resolved in the time of Augustine with the condemnation of the optimistic Celtic monk. However, Pelagius, like most Irish monks, would not remain silent, and he came back again in many different forms to haunt his adversaries, most notably, of course, in the troubled, well-meaning, sentimental form of Jean Jacques Rousseau. Human nature, argued Rousseau, is fundamentally good, but wherever we see it, it acts bad. Why? Because "they" have bound human nature in chains, which have made it bad. The referent of "they" would change through the years, but the charge would not.

So questions about the nature of human nature and the progress of the human species are firmly planted in the intellectual consciousness of the Western world; and though there is little reason to think they will ever be satisfactorily resolved, there is also little reason to think that the Western variety of humankind can stop talking about them or stop arranging and rearranging its social order to fit the way it responds to those questions at various times. To the extent that the rest of the world is influenced by Western mentality, or at least by its vocabulary, the same questions will be asked—though they do not arise naturally in the Islamic heritage, for example.*

I have chosen the two vectors, "modernization" and "human nature," around which I arranged my presentation, rather arbitrarily. But there are solid historical and intellectual reasons for choosing such an arrangement. The principal question seems to me to be not whether one should use those two vectors but whether one should add a third or even a fourth, as my colleague David Tracy has suggested. I do not do so, because as soon as one gets beyond a two-by-two table, my capacity to juggle intellectual complexities declines to virtually zero. A secondary reason is that the vectors Tracy recommends would not substantially modify the paradigm of ideologies that I am using, though his insights do enrich the paradigm, and because they do I shall summarize briefly in this

---

* The happy compromise arrived at in many Islamic countries is to opt for Western "socialism" combined with "traditional" Islam. The juxtaposition of West and East in these solutions may be uneasy (see, for example, the description of various styles of compromise in Clifford Geertz's *Islam Observed* [New Haven: Yale University Press, 1969]); but then human beings are quite skillful at combining very disparate answers and even very disparate questions in provisional ideologies. For how many generations such juxtapositions can continue is another question. I think one would be ill advised to bet against such provisional ideologies continuing for a long time.

chapter Tracy's thinking. I refer to it frequently in this book and would suggest that the reader consult Tracy's own volume, when it appears, for his developed thought.*

Tracy uses two principal tools in his analysis: "visions of ultimate reality" (or what I call "styles of religious reflection") and "understanding the meanings and relationship of justice and love." The Protestant imagination, he contends, is dialectical and proceeds through the logic of contradiction and negation, exulting in such paradoxical if not contradictory terms as "the crucified God." The Catholic imagination, on the other hand, uses the logic-ordered relationships that are arranged around a chosen focal meaning. Thus the Catholic imagination theologically rejoices in such analogical symbols as "the mystical body" and transfers its symbols to its social thinking by understanding society as an "organism" analogous to the human body.

It should be quite clear that if one views society as an analogue to an organism, that is to say, as a sustained network of relationships, the combination of love with careful concern for justice is not only possible but necessary. If one approaches society from a dialectical viewpoint, however, in which individual struggles with individual and each individual struggles against society, then one both logically and psychologically sees substantial conflict between self-sacrificing love, on the one hand, and justice, on the other. If one views reconciliation as the most natural as well as the most admirable form of human social behavior, one is well served by a justice transformed by love; if, on the other hand, one sees society as an arena of contradiction, negation, and conflict, one is well served by an approach that encourages some to seek rough justice and others to heedless self-sacrifice, some to the quest for what is legitimately their rights, others to necessary obligation to expiate in guilt for injustice whether they were responsible for it or not.

Thus, when one is faced with the question of race in the

* My summary is based on conversations with Tracy and attendance at his seminar presentations. It certainly does not reveal the full scope of of his thinking, but he was kind enough to review my remarks before publication and granted them if not an *imprimatur* at least a *nihil obstat.*

United States, the Catholic propensity would be to urge on both black and white the need not to expiate for the injustices of the past but to arrive at just solutions to the present problems, while at the same time abandoning past hatreds and prejudices to become reconciled in generous mutual forgiveness, one with another. The Protestant predisposition, I think, is to urge upon blacks the stern, unforgiving pursuit of a justice denied in the past and on whites the need to expiate for the past by heedless self-sacrifice in the present.

"Can you really expect blacks to love whites?" I was asked once. My response was that if they were followers of Jesus of Nazareth, yes, they could legitimately be expected to maintain a posture of loving reconciliation while at the same time seek that which is justly theirs. I suspect that would be an answer much more difficult for a Protestant to give.

Both Catholic and Protestant ethical theory (save for the right-wing fundamentalist Protestants) come down in relatively the same position in a two-by-two table created by the vectors of "modernization" and the "nature of human nature." Both reject modern society, and both reject the easy assumption that human nature can be remade, which is shared by the socialists, the Freudians, and the anarchists. However, within their own quadrant, there are, it should be clear from our discussion here, major differences between Protestant and Catholic social ideology. They differ, as we shall see in greater detail later, in their fundamental view of the nature of human nature. The Catholic ideology is willing to give the benefit of a doubt (however slight at times) to humankind's fundamental goodness; the Protestant ideology is more disposed to question humankind's fundamental goodness. Moreover, Catholic theory sees society as an organic network, whereas Protestant theory is inclined to see it as a process of isolated individuals (though Calvin and Niebuhr, in this respect, would be somewhat more "communal" than the Lutherans). Also, though most Protestant social ethical theories of the day are severely critical of anomic, alienated, modernized society and would therefore belong in the same quadrant as Catholics, they are more likely to be critical of it because of its oppressions and its inhumanity and not because they see it violating the fundamental organic nature of social relationships, as do Catholics.

More than this must be said, albeit tentatively. Talcott Parsons, interpreting but still relying on Max Weber, argues that Lutheranism finally freed the individual from the constraints of traditional hierarchical authority and greatly facilitated, if it did not cause, the modernization process. Modernization, then, according to Parsons, both as a theory and as a phenomenon, springs from the Reformation. Contemporary Protestant social theorists may reject the evils of modernization and they may dispute (quite properly, it seems to me), whether there is a causal connection between the Reformation and modernization. However, I think they must face the fact that an "affinity" does exist. It is clear, at least in his later life, that that is all Max Weber meant by linking the Protestant ethic and the spirit of capitalism.

Furthermore, both the capitalist and socialist theories grew up in the atmosphere of late-eighteenth- and early-nineteenth-century Protestantism and were shaped by the intellectual environment of Lockean individualism and Hobbesian pessimism, both of which, however indirectly, derived from the individualistic Protestantism of the era. The relationships are complicated and sometimes obscure, and I have no desire to make too much of the point; but subject to clarification by the historians of ideas, one can say at a high level of generality that capitalism and socialism are Protestant heresies, however much Protestant ethicians of that day and this may be offended by the abuses of capitalism (or socialism, too, for that matter). The capitalist utilitarian ethic maintains Protestant pessimism about human nature. Marx, influenced by Rousseau through the French Revolution, would argue the possibility of the liberation of human nature from the chains of bondage and oppression, introducing just enough of Kant through Hegel to insist on the inherent moral, not to say messianic, obligation of this liberation. To top things off, Marx would add, in one of the most attractive and elegant ideological paradigms ever developed, that the progress toward liberation was an inevitable historical development (a notion which nineteenth-century liberal capitalism would absorb from a very different source through Charles Darwin).

The principal goal of this book is to delineate a Catholic social ideology, and I shall do so by comparing it with capitalist, socialist, and anarchist ideologies. By way of schematic conclusion, in terms of both criticism and practical programming, there is in this ecumenical age a substantial similarity between the Protestant and Catholic Christian response to most practical issues. They differ in three major matters: (1) the classical Protestant tradition approaches to justice and love with a very different perspective than the traditional Catholic position; (2) Protestants and Catholics have fundamentally different perspectives of the nature of human nature and the nature of human society; (3) for reasons of both history and theory there are certain links between Protestantism and capitalism and socialism that do not exist between Catholicism and those two ideologies. However, it might be noted in passing that it is also true that there are links between Catholicism and Proudhonian and Roszakian anarchism that do not exist between anarchism and Protestantism. If Marx was a Protestant heretic, Proudhon was a Catholic heretic. R. H. Tawney was wrong: Karl Marx was not the last of the Schoolmen; despite himself, Theodore Roszak is.

CHAPTER 3

ᖇ ᖇ ᖇ

Modernization

SOMETHING tremendously important happened between 1500 and 1900: there was a major change in human living in the Western world and, ultimately, in the remainder of the world. Indeed, sociology as a discipline came into existence precisely as a reaction to that change, and a reflection upon it. Only, in truth, we do not altogether understand the change. Our attempts to describe it, much less to explain it, despite all the intellectual energy expended since Auguste Comte, have been less than completely successful. And the more social and historical data become available to us, the more baffled we are about exactly what did happen and why. I shall argue in this book that modernization, as it is characteristically and implicitly understood, is rejected both on theoretical principles by the Catholic social ideology and by much of the available empirical evidence. "Modernization," as the term is usually understood, is not only wrong as a norm, it is also inaccurate as a description. However, there is a very real danger that my position will be understood as denying that anything happened at all between 1500 and 1900. The modernization model, I shall contend, does not adequately fit the data, and we desperately need a new model. But the attractiveness, not to say seductiveness, of the modernization model comes from the very fact that it does fit very well some of the data that are immediately obvious to everyone, and at one time seemed to fit a lot of other data. Part of the problem those of us who are uneasy with it have is that any alternatives we come up with lack the elegance, the simplicity, and even the explanatory power of the modernization model.

It has become part of the collective preconscious of the Western world; it is reinforced by all the evolutionary theories—Marxist, Comteian, Darwinian, and Christian—all of which owe something to the fourteenth-century mystical visionary Joachim de Flora, who was in his own way a direct lineal descendant of Augustine.* To question the modernization model is a difficult if not impossible task, because even if one wins some telling points, one is unable to dislodge the picture from the preconscious of the other in the dialogue. Even the most sophisticated social scientist is apt to respond something like, "Science and technology make large corporate bureaucracies necessary, don't they?" The answer is, I think, no, in fact they don't. Historically, bureaucratization and technology have been linked, but the link is by no means necessary or inevitable. The point will be accepted by some, but the picture is not dislodged; science and technology mean the great factory, the huge machine, the large corporation, and the picture remains intact, indestructible forever.

Science, of course, is merely the understanding of the way things work, and technology is merely the application of science to practical problems. Medical science and medical technology, it is now clear, do not require large hospitals, and have made their major contributions to the prolongation of human life through relatively simple public-health measures that do not require large machines. Some large hospitals may be necessary, and for certain relatively infrequent problems that affect individuals large machines may be necessary or useful; but the general life expectancy of a population is not

---

* Consider the propensity of the various evolutionary thinkers to use three stages: medieval, bourgeois, and socialist for Marx; Catholic, Protestant, and sociological for Comte; and Father, Son, and Holy Spirit for the Abbot Joachim.

notably enhanced by kidney machines or sophisticated computer diagnosis—as grateful as we may be for such innovations when they may delay or prevent a particular death at a given time. Indeed, the scientific discovery of the link between cigarette smoking and cancer and the technology of discouraging or preventing the inhalation of carcinogens are probably much more important for improving life expectancy than are large hospitals and big machines.

Science and technology, in other words, may well necessitate some large machines and some big corporations (though hardly U.S. Steel and General Motors), but science and technology do not by themselves necessarily demand bigness either in the tool or in the human organization that uses it. We can have practically all the benefits of the scientific and technological society without nearly so many large corporate organizations or even so many big tools. For example, it is now generally agreed that one needs neither the tractor nor the collective farm (or alternatively the agricultural corporation) to resolve the world's food problem. In his brilliant article "Myths of the Food Crisis,"[1] Nick Eberstadt summarizes the facts of science and technology in food production:

> You don't need tractors, spray planes, and other trappings of the Green Revolution to raise yields. With know-how and little else (a few simple hand tools, some good seeds, a little pesticide, manure, or fertilizer) a diligent but poor farmer can produce at least one crop a year with yields higher than those now harvested in rich countries.
>
> This is not easy but it can be done. . . . Poor countries, moreover, are tropical countries. With an investment in irrigation and drainage, which in most cases pays for itself in less than two years, the poor farmer can be harvesting three crops a year to our one.[2]

Eberstadt's point should be shattering to our "pictures." Theoretical knowledge, which is science, and the practical knowledge, which is technology, not only do not require machines and large organizations, but they can get in the way. Science and technology without the machines and the large corporations could not only solve the food problems of most poor countries but also produce large food surpluses for the whole human race. Our emphasis on size and the machine may well have brought us down the wrong path. The myth of modernization, in this respect at least, may not only have been counterproductive but destructive.

One may enthusiastically accept Eberstadt's analysis and still not perceive what a devastating critique it is of the modernization picture that is so much a part of the vector-creating symbols in our preconscious. Thus, as Christopher Lasch has pointed out in his thoughtful review of recent scholarship on the history of the family,[3] there is precious little support for the modernization image in that literature, yet virtually all the historians in this specialty cling to the model—including Edward Shorter, in his brilliantly speculative *The Making of the Modern Family*.[4] It turns out that the extended family was very rare at the beginning of the American republic, and the nuclear family was almost as typical then as it is now. Still, editor Michael Gordon, in the introduction to his book, *The American Family in Social-Historical Perspective*,[5] feels constrained not merely to discuss modernization but to fall back on Robert Nisbet's modernization model (as brilliantly described in *The Sociological Tradition*[6]) to explain what "has happened" to the American family.

Similarly, in Peter Laslett's *Household and Family in Past Time*,[7] there is overwhelming evidence that the English family, for at least three centuries, has been nuclear in structure. Indeed, the various researchers who contributed to the volume are hard put to find any evidence of the extended family at all in the areas of western Europe that had research data available. J. Goody sums it up:

> I have tried to establish that it is not only for England that we need to abandon the myth of the 'extended family'—as the term is often understood. In one form or another this myth has haunted historical and comparative studies since the time of Maine and Fustel de Coulanges, whether the work has been undertaken by historians, sociologists or anthropologists. Whatever the shape of the kin groups of earlier societies, none were undifferentiated communities of the kind beloved by nine-

teenth century theorists, Marxist and non-Marxist alike. Units of production were everywhere relatively small, kin-based units; differences in size and context are important in the comparative study of the family, but they should never obscure the basic similarities in the way that domestic groups are organized throughout the whole range of human societies.[8]

Now the notion of the declining power of the extended kin group is one of the major premises of the modernization hypothesis. Demographic historians have virtually destroyed that assumption (thereby raising a variety of interesting and as yet unanswered questions about the variability of family behavior, a variability that does not seem to fit any simple or even complex evolutionary model); yet they still seem constrained to pay lip service to the modernization picture. In Lasch's words, "It is hard to give up a picture of the family which suggests . . . that earlier generations were incapable of understanding things we now take for granted, that they seldom attained our heights of feeling; that love, sex and personal autonomy are our own inventions. . . ."[9]*

Historical research shows then that the nuclear family long antedated the Industrial Revolution, and that for that matter, the Protestant ethic was to be found in late medieval Florence, long before Martin Luther. Women had more freedom and more equal rights than they did in the Roman Empire. Individualism, of a sort at least, flourished within the Roman Empire, and both agnosticism and atheism (to say nothing of hypocrisy) were scarcely the results of the Enlightenment. Still, having made all these observations, something did happen between 1500 and 1900.

Nisbet in the *Sociological Tradition* summarizes the contributions of the sociological greats—Tönnies, Weber, Marx, Durkheim, Simmel—to the modernization thesis. One could

---

* The data in the Gordon book gives very little supporting evidence to the notion of a "sexual revolution" or a rise of sexual permissiveness. Data assembled by Phillips Cutright also suggest that the sexual revolution is as false a myth as the modernization model. Some things have changed, perhaps; but Shorter's speculation about not one but two sexual revolutions (one in the early eighteenth century and one in the middle twentieth) may be ingenious but goes far beyond his data.

TABLE I.
Approaches to "Modernization"

Parsons, *et al.*	Institutional differentiation; separation of abstract and emotion, effect on child-rearing through differentiation of roles of parents; emergence of autonomous individual operating freely (Protestant); universal, specific, rational-achievement behavior replacing particularistic, diffuse, nonrational, ascriptive behavior
Cooley	Decline of the "primary" group
Tönnies, *et al.*	Movement from "ethnic" to universalist (from "community" to "association," from kin to contract)
Becker, *et al.*	Movement from sacred to secular
Redfield	Movement from folk to urban
Patterson	Movement from "ethnic" to universalist
Slater and Bennis	Emergence of transient man in temporary society
Luckmann	Emergence of belief systems and resultant behavior patterns functional for large corporate bodies (old systems—family, religion—may survive in "interstices")
Rostow	Arrival at economic takeoff point
Nisbet	Decline in community, authority, status, and the sacred, leading to alienation
Shorter	Breakdown of family constraints
Bell	Rise of bourgeois economic impulse and cultural modernity

add such American writers as Cooley, Becker, Redfield, Luckmann, and Rostow (see Table I). Talcott Parsons and his colleagues and students have provided the most elaborate (if not always the clearest) description of the modernization phenomenon. The Reformation freed the individual from the rigid controls of the medieval society, and the newly independent and mobile individuals began to explore—the far reaches of the globe, the internal depths of the personality, the complexities of the world around them, and the various possibilities of the new scientific knowledge that their exploration made possible. A multiplier effect set in, and knowledge, technology, mobility, and innovation accelerated the speed of development. New institutions emerged to make use of the knowledge, technology, and freedom, which rapidly differentiated among themselves, acquiring more and more specific functions. The state bureaucracies, the mercantile organization (such as the East India Company), and then the manufacturing and transportation corporation emerged to handle functions that either had not existed previously or had been taken care of by the Church and the family in much less elaborate fashion. These two latter institutions had at one time vast and undifferentiated powers and functions, but gradually yielded most of them to the new specific institutions. The family began to focus specifically on the provision of emotional satisfaction to the spouses and the socialization of the children, yielding virtually all of its productive and economic functions to the new corporations. The church gradually limited its role to dealing with eschatological issues and yielded its legal, economic, and welfare roles to new institutions or to the growing state bureaucracies.

At the same time, according to Parsons and some of his disciples, differentiation of roles and the division of labor within the family rapidly emerged. In the premodernized world there were relatively few distinctions between the roles of husband and wife; both performed relatively similar economic and child-rearing functions. However, with modernization the husband became the specialist in abstract, task-oriented leadership in the family and the wife a specialist in socioemotional leadership. This led to a situation in which the child had to internalize two kinds of parent—the abstract parent and the loving parent. In resolving the tension between those two, there emerged a personality with both the need and the ability to break even more decisively with the traditions of the past. Such a personality could no longer accept the hierarchical sacred authority that demanded not only obedience but also emotional dependency. The new personality would not depend on "pre-Oedipal authority" but would rather identify with internalized "Oedipal authority." Modern man had come into existence.

All very neat, plausible, and reasonable. It seems to fit so much of what we know in the world today. Unfortunately, it is extremely difficult to link such a model with the detailed historical data that are becoming available, especially since it is now apparent that different groups have followed different paths to modernity. The Italian family, for example, seems to have maintained a very different husband-wife relationship in their American experience than did many other immigrant family groups. The Italian wife is a person of considerable importance within her family system and has some areas of absolute authority, but because her virtue is of such sacred and compelling importance in Italian culture, the husband and sons are most reluctant to let the wife and daughters work outside the family environment for any sustained period of time. Thus, even in comparison with the Poles, who came at roughly the same time, it would appear that Italian women were much less likely to enter the industrial occupational force and more likely to engage in "home work" such as making clothes or curtains or taking in boarders. Presumably, such a rigid approach to family life would impede Americanization and social mobility, but in fact it would appear that such behavior patterns—remarkably tenacious, even among Italian upper-middle-class suburbanites—provided the Italian family structure with much greater resilience in the face of the traumas of immigration. It produced less family disorganization and actually facilitated Italian upward mobility, so that at the present time, Italians—thought still relatively recent arrivals—are the third wealthiest religio-ethnic group in the United States (behind Jews and Irish Catholics). So one must ask, then, which family structure is the more "modernized," is it the more differentiated, the more mobile?

Still, one cannot read the authors listed and briefly described in Table I without concluding that they are on to something, though it is hard to say precisely what. Part of the difficulty of trying to contest with the modernization assumption is that in the process of discussing it, meaning seems to shift, as is natural whenever a treasured picture is under assault. Thus I have tried to set down schematically in Table II my understanding of the modernization model so that the reader will be able to judge for himself what I mean when I say that capitalism and socialism accept modernization and Catholicism and anarchism reject it.

TABLE II.
Modernization Model

As Description	As Norm to Be Rejected*
1. Modernization frees individual from ties and obligations imposed by accidents of birth, leading to personal autonomy and maturity and social and territorial mobility, e.g., ties of geography, ethnic group, religion, family of origin, occupational inheritance, political traditions, hereditary and sacral authority, and, more recently, sexual role definition.	1. Loss of support provided by old times—lonely crowd, one-dimensional man.
2. Family life marked by romantic love, emotional intimacy, nonauthoritarian socialization, and awareness of needs of children.	2. Trap of bourgeois marriage.
3. Assumption by specific institutions (usually large, formal, and bureaucratic) of roles formerly played by undifferentiated family and Church.	3. Role diffusion because of inconsistent demands.
4. Organization of institutions of "rational," "scientific," and bureaucratic principles instead of sacred or hereditary symbols.	4. Alienation, normlessness, rootlessness.
5. Interaction partners (economic, political, sexual, neighborhood, etc.) chosen on the basis of personal decision—presumed to be rational, individual, and career oriented.	5. Mass society, oppression of individual by "system."
6. Personality characterized by self-control, deferred gratification, independent decision-making (identification with and internalization of Oedipal authority) as opposed to impulsive, emotional, dependent, labile personality (dependence on pre-Oedipal authority).	6. Inability to give self in trust, openness, intimacy.
7. As a result, notable decline in importance of intimate, personal, informal, nonrational, local, permanent, loyalty-based relationships—both to individuals and to social systems.	7. Quest for community.

* Defenders of modernization often simultaneously depict it as a "description" (the way things have been and are) and a "norm" (the way they must be or ought to be, e.g., Orlando Patterson). Critics generally accept it as a description (though not Lasch), but question it as a norm or an ideal. Some (like me) question its adequacy as a description. Catholic theory would doubt its ability to describe because Catholic theory doubts that point number 7 can happen. Anarchists in general would not doubt its desirability but would question its possibility.

A second difficulty in discussing modernization is that one never knows when the description will turn into prescription. As most Americans are committed to the notion that evolutionary progress is good and since modernization is a description of the evolutionary process, what is described in the first column of Table II often seems to be an account not only of what has happened but also of what should have happened and a norm for what ought to continue to happen. Orlando Patterson surely assumes that modernization has occurred, is occurring, and ought to continue to occur. Anarchists and similar thinkers (including some New Leftists such as political scientist John Schaar) are prepared to concede that the modernization model as depicted in Table II has occurred, but will disagree vigorously that it ought to have occurred and insist strongly that it ought not to be permitted to continue to occur. Their criticisms of modernization as a normative model are presented in the second column of Table II. The Catholic theory, I will suggest in a later chapter, rejects the modernization model both as a description and as a prescription.

The modernization model sees the process as beginning (however and whenever that might have been) by freeing the individual from the nonrational ties and obligations imposed by birth and providing him with personal autonomy and maturity and then, as a result, with social and territorial mobility. As modernization occurs, in other words, the individual is freed from ties of place, tribe, faith, ancestral family, parent-chosen occupation, the authority of Church, parent, and traditional political leadership, and now even from the ties of traditional sexual role definition.

Such a modernized person is raised in a family characterized by romantic love, emotional intimacy (between spouses and between parents and children), open and permissive child-rearing, and sensitivity to the needs of children. When he reaches maturity, the modernized person re-creates the family of his childhood and obtains from it the psychic and emotional satisfaction necessary to sustain him when he enters the formalized, bureaucratized, rationalized, universalized, and more recently, computerized system of specific institutions by which the modern commercial and industrial world continues to operate and to produce the wealth that makes an affluent and abundant family life possible. These institutions, in their turn, are organized scientifically and rationally on the premise that all that is required from the individual participant is the effective and responsible exercise of the particular and specific occupational skills he brings to the organization, so that the organization may achieve its own limited and specific goals.*

Though the most fundamental emotional and psychic needs are to be derived from the interpersonal intimacy of the family, it is still assumed that behavior in the world of the corporate institution has, at least for better-educated people, a possibility of producing compellingly attractive need satisfactions. The familial intimacy is perhaps taken for granted, and the difference between success and failure is measured by achievement in the world of career. So despite the emphasis of Parsons and others (including a whole generation of American novelists) on the fundamental importance of sexual fulfillment and intimacy, the major emphasis of the feminist movement, in fact if not in theory, has not been on better family lives or richer personal intimacy but on career satisfaction. The family and the Church, Luckmann tells us, operate in the interstices of life, which have been left vacant by the large corporate bureaucracies.[10]

Whether career success or family fulfillment is more important may be a moot point. The career is of considerable importance, especially for the well-educated segment of society, and interaction partners—economic, political, recreational, even to some extent sexual—are chosen not only on the basis of personal decision but also to a very considerable extent on a rational consideration of how such ties may contribute to one's career success in the corporate institutions. Such an autonomous, rational, individualistic, career-oriented individual is well disciplined, emotionally well controlled, self-actualizing, and motivated by the internal satisfactions of success more than he is by pleasure, honor, and other such nonrational and impulsive emotions.

* In Japan the corporation may play a far more paternalistic and familial role than it does in the United States, but that is taken to be a peculiarity of Japanese culture.

When one ponders such a description of modern human-kind, one must say that there are doubtless people one knows who pretty much fit such a paradigm. They are members of the national elites for the most part—professors at the great universities, executives in the large national corporations, administrators in the upper levels of the governmental bu-reaucracies. If the scholars who write about modern man take it for granted that the person described in the first six steps of my model (see Table II) is indeed modern man, the reason may well be that in the environment in which they live and work, many, if not most people, are to some extent character-ized by such attributes and styles. The extent to which such attributes and styles mark other people in a large, industri-alized nation as the United States (presumably the most modernized in the world) is open to question or is at least a matter for further specification by research. The nonacademic or the nonelite might be tempted to look around his neighbor-hood and say, "There's not many of those folk living here."

But the first six steps in the model are only a prelude to the seventh proposition, which is, I think, the basic if not always the explicit premise in the discussion of modernization. It is, at any rate, the statement of the modernization continuum that I intend to discuss—and ultimately deny.*

The human being who has emerged from the modernization process, it is assumed, will differ from his ancestor (at what-ever point in the past one wishes to say was just prior to the beginning of modernization) in that he places much less im-portance than did his ancestor in intimate, personal, informal, nonrational, local, permanent, loyalty-based relationships both to individuals and to social systems. As the free, autonomous, rational human being, he is not tied down by such archaic, premodern, sacred, ethnic ties.

---

* Another proposition that might parallel number seven in Table II would be that modern humans, because of their mobility, their ration-ality, and their autonomy, no longer need the sacred. Hence they are increasingly and progressively dispensing with the need for religious symbols to cope with ultimate questions of the meaning of life and the universe. There is, I would suggest, even less data to support such a proposition, but I discuss that subject in my book *Unsecular Man* (New York: Schocken Books, 1972).

Part of the immense appeal of the modernization model is its evolutionary and progressive character. It purports to represent the wave of history, the natural working out of forces of development making for fuller and freer human life. Modernization is the future triumphing over the past; it is the way things should be and in fact the way things are going to be because inevitable historical processes are at work ensuring the final success of modernization. One jumps on board the train for the future before it pulls out of the Transylvania station. The modernization model flatters our pride: we are better than those who went before us. It satisfies our need to be in the advance guard: we are the way those who come after us will be. For many semieducated moderns, these twin appeals are enough for them to buy the modernization model without a second thought.

But note how often and how persuasively this sort of argument has been used—by Comte, Marx, the social Darwinists, Margaret Mead, Alvin Toffler, B. F. Skinner, Charles Reich, and more recently by George C. Lodge in his book, *The New American Ideology* (New York, Alfred A. Knopf, 1975). If one presents a policy or a program or an ideology as a historical inevitable because of the evolutionary forces at work, one has already made a large number of converts.

It was, after all, the same sort of argument Augustine used for buying a one-way ticket to the City of God. Only it ought not to be confused with social or historical science.

I will suggest in later chapters that capitalism and socialism, at least in their classic statements, assume that such is the description of modern man as he is or as he ought to be, and the involvement of modernized countries in modernizing other countries ought to be such as to facilitate the emergence of a class of people (called middle class if you're a capitalist, or party members if you are socialist) marked by such characteristics. I will also contend that the Catholic and anarchist ideologies both find such modern humans to be morally and aesthetically unattractive. They consider it bad enough that a number of them exist in the North Atlantic world and appalling that the West should try to impose such personality types on the rest of humankind. The Catholic ideology, in addition, will argue on the basis of experience that such rootless, alienated individuals may not be humanly healthy and that a society dominated by them will be a sick society. It would further argue on the basis of experience that it does not, thank God, know very many such people.

But if modernization has not produced the process schematized in Table II, what then has happened? After all, even I have admitted that something has happened.

We need a new model. There is not enough data yet to delineate such a model, but my own hunch goes something like this: The determining factor of the modern world was the development of applied science and technology which resulted in the production of a sufficient amount of abundance to ensure the prolonging of human life and a rapidly expanding population. The context which made these developments possible was the emergence of a social order in late medieval Europe that maintained some internal peace and security from external invasion facilitated by a period of time free from natural disasters like the bubonic plague. The overarching cause was Christianity, at that time a peculiar combination of Hebrew religion, Greek philosophy, Roman law, and Celtic mysticism, a time that we characterize now as the early Middle Ages.

The belief in history as process rather than cycle, the assumption that the universe is purposeful and hence understandable, the conviction that God transcends and is superior to the secular world, and the equal conviction that humankind's vocation is to serve God's plan by vigorous action in the secular world are all uniquely Christian notions; they led to the conclusion that science is not merely for knowledge but also for action. Professor Lynn White is quite correct when he argues that the material universe, when deprived of its pervasively sacred character, was opened not only to human use but to human exploitation and even destruction.[11] Such diverse scholars as Tonybee, Mumford, and the authors of the Meadows Report, *The Limits to Growth*,[12] could thus blame with some show of plausibility the ecological, environmental problems on Christianity—conveniently forgetting that another aspect of Christian doctrine demanded respect for the world, which if it was no longer divine was still a "sacrament," a revelation of the divine.

As a student insisted during a seminar discussion of this subject, "If you introduce technical innovation into a traditional society, something is going to happen to the established pattern of relationships." Doubtless the first metal-tipped plow, wielded by some Frisian farmer in the ninth century, White tells us, turned Frisian society on its ears; but such social change is merely change and not necessarily progress or necessarily regress either. More important for the issue at hand, and what remains to be proved, is that either technological innovation or the resulting social change necessarily produces the decline of personal relationships of the sort described in the seventh proposition of Table II. Technological innovation and the resulting social changes *may* produce a decline in such relationships, and for some individuals and groups under some historical circumstances they may have in fact produced a decline; but I would contend that decline is not inevitable, that if in fact it has occurred for some people at some times is a matter for empirical research and not a priori theoretical assumption.

CHAPTER 4
ꝗ ꝗ ꝗ

Models of
Human Nature

A WRITER for *The Christian Century* and a staff member of the National Council of Churches recently came back from the now almost obligatory tour of Communist China with the joyous announcement that the Maoists were better Christians than most Christians and that they were producing a new kind of human being, one who was self-sacrificing, communitarian, and more concerned about the welfare of the whole society than about his own private good. There was no particular evidence that the gentleman in question planned to migrate immediately to this marvelous "Christian" society, but he could not restrain the lyricism with which he sang its praises.

I will lay aside pertinent questions about how thorough his exploration of the new China really was, whether it really was a new China that he had observed or merely the old China with peace and order established, or whether he had also visited Singapore or Taiwan to see what kind of economic miracle can be created by the same Chinese culture under capitalism. But I really must ask one critical question: What the hell kind of Protestant is he if he thinks human nature can be remade? Even Martin Luther didn't think that.

However, the gentleman was probably not reporting as a Protestant but rather as a descendant of Jean Jacques Rousseau and his Enlightenment optimism about the reformation of human nature. Nineteenth-century liberalism and romanticism, as well as twentieth-century anarchism, socialism, Behaviorism, and neo-Freudianism, are all convinced that human nature is fundamentally good and that humankind engages in evil behavior because of oppression or ignorance or some kind of tyranny that is presently to be found in the social structure. If you correct the oppressive structures, you will have remade human nature and eliminated much of the evil and the suffering in the world. All such models of human nature are Pelagian or semi-Pelagian—and hence I subsume them under the Pelagian half of the Augustinian conscience. They do not deny the existence of a basic flaw in human nature as we find it (their equivalent of the Christian original sin), but they believe that salvation is both possible and available with relative ease if one can reform or remake the structures of society (see Table III). There may be a difficult generation or two while the effects of the socialization process that occurred under the old unjust structures are undone, but after that, salvation of one sort or another is assured.

The closest thing to an out-and-out Pelagian today is the famous linguist from the Massachusetts Institute of Technology, Professor Noam Chomsky, who in his *Reflection on Language* argues with his customary vigor and clarity an extremely optimistic position about human nature. Chomsky begins by refuting the assumption that "Empiricism and later behaviorist psychology are firmly grounded in the doctrine that there is no nontrivial theory of human nature."[1*]

Chomsky's linguistic analysis has discovered (apparently) a universal grammar, a language faculty within the cognitive capacity that seems to be a biological given of the human

---

* Since my book assumes that the issue is nontrivial and argues that the present swing to Manichaean pessimism results fundamentally from the resurfacing of the question, there is no need here to repeat Chomsky's argument. However, it is certainly one of the most effective analyses of the link between environmentalism and political liberalism that has yet been written—a link which Chomsky argues, very persuasively it seems to me, is a philosophical as well as a political mistake.

condition. We are born not with just an amorphous capacity to learn language but with a highly structured capability of imposing grammar on reality. There are, Chomsky argues, probably other such innate capacities and systems—perhaps closely linked (though Chomsky himself does not state it) with Clifford Geertz's templates. Human creativity is thus "predicated upon a system of rules and forms, in part determined by intrinsic human capacities. Without such constraints, we have arbitrary and random behavior, not creative acts. The constructions of common sense and scientific inquiry derive no less from principles grounded in the structure of the human mind."[2]

Admitting that it is a big leap, Chomsky nonetheless suggests that "It is reasonable to suppose that just as intrinsic structures of mind underlie the development of cognitive structures, so a 'species character' provides the framework for the growth of moral consciousness, cultural achievement, and even participation in a free and just community."[3] And there is still another leap: "It is, to be sure, a great intellectual leap from observations on the basis for cognitive development to particular conclusions on the laws of our nature and the conditions for their fulfillment; say, to the conclusion that human needs and capacities will find their fullest expression in a society of free and creative producers, working in a system of free association in which 'social bonds' will replace 'all fetters in human society.' "[4]

So beginning with universal grammar, Chomsky argues to a fundamental structure of human nature that raises the possibility of a situation in which "No longer repressed and distorted by competitive and authoritarian social structures, these passions and instincts may set the stage for a new scientific civilization in which 'animal nature' is transcended and human nature can truly flourish."[5]

Chomsky says, quite correctly, that there is an important intellectual tradition that antedates his position. He is searching for "deeper roots in rationalist efforts to establish a theory of human freedom." It is fair to say that this swing of the pendulum in the Manichaean direction makes Chomsky something of a voice crying in the wilderness—just now, at any rate.

Freud himself was relatively little concerned about social reform and profoundly pessimistic about human nature; but the neo-Freudians, particularly Erich Fromm, seemed convinced that the neurosis-producing socialization experiences are caused for the most part by the oppression of capitalist social structures. Eliminate capitalism, replace it with socialism, and dependency relationships will diminish notably; authenticity, autonomy, and maturity will spread rapidly throughout the society. However, Fromm and other Freudian socialists have had to hedge their bets, because there is no reason to believe that neurosis has declined substantially in any existing socialist state. So when they speak of socialism, they have in mind not so much the socialism that actually exists but a kind of ideal socialist society that, if it existed, would tend to produce a non-neurotic human nature. Such a vision is an extremely useful rhetorical device, because one can refuse to assume responsibility for any existing society on the grounds that such societies don't fit one's vision. The socialism pure and undefiled that will remake human nature cannot be found presently in the world and indeed probably never will be found in the world.

The nonsocialist Freudians, whatever their political predispositions, are forced to take a much less systemwide approach. They talk about therapy as a cure for individual dependency relationships and a therapeutic ethic that guides social policymakers, administrators, and social workers in their dealings with the disadvantaged persons in the society.

Just as the socialist world view has influenced Freudians, so most socialists outside the so-called socialist countries have a good strong dose of Freud mixed with their Marx. Their emphasis may be more structural and interpersonal, but it is no accident that *The Wretched of the Earth* was written by a psychiatrist.

The principal difference between the socialists and the anarchists in their respective models of human nature is that the latter apparently consider human nature, even in its present flawed form, to be fundamentally social. You do not have

TABLE III.
Models of Human Nature

	Basic Nature	Social Inclination	Flaw	Remark-ability	Freedom to Choose	Salvation	Social Action Propensity
Pelagian	good	not recorded	none	yes	yes	hard work, use of own talents	none
Neo-Pelagian (Chomsky)	good	social	ignorance	yes	yes	rationality	republic led by wise and virtuous
Neo-Freudian (Fromm)	good	potentially social, now antisocial	dependency relations	yes	not now	authenticity, autonomy, maturity	"therapeutic" ethic
Socialism	good	potentially social, now antisocial	economic structures	yes	not now	revolution, liberation socialist state = new economic structures	concentration of power in agents of the people (state)
Anarchism (Roszak)	good	social	society, technology, affluence	yes	not now	end of society as we know it	withdrawal from affluent, technical society
Behaviorism (Skinner)	good	individualist, aggressive, etc.	bad conditioning	yes	no way!	better conditioning	Walden Two run by "conditioners"
Liberalism* (Rousseau, Jefferson)	good	now-individualist, aggressive—but not necessarily so	ignorance, tyranny	yes	yes	knowledge and freedom (whether you want it or not)	New Deal, welfare state
Romantic (Stendhal, Goode, Norman O. Brown)	good	social (but usually dyadic)	excessive rationality	yes	yes	release of sentiment, feeling, polymorphous perversity	sensibility, emotionalism (politics of gestures) withdrawal into romantic hole

⎰ SEMI-PELAGIAN ⎱

TABLE III. (continued)
Models of Human Nature

	Basic Nature	Social Inclination	Flaw	Remak-ability	Freedom to Choose	Salvation	Social Action Propensity
Manichaeanism	bad	individualist, aggressive	body	no	no	escape from the body	none
Neo-Manichaeanism (Heilbroner)	hopeless	fearful	human fear, selfishness, prejudice	no	no	stoic resignation	none
Lutheran	bad	individualist, aggressive	sin	no	not much	trust in God's forgiveness	two kingdoms
Niebuhr*	bad	individualist, aggressive	sin	no	not much	heroic personal effort, social and political reform (but expect much less than liberals)	correction of injustice, reparation, expiation
Conservative (Burke, Bell)	flawed	weakly social	irrationality, hubris	not really	some	maintenance of social order	ambivalent gradualism
Capitalism	aggressive	self-seeking	too much regulation	no	yes	competition, market-place, scientific management	"utilitarian" ethic, good of the corporation
Ethologism-socio-biologism (Lorenz, Wilson)	aggressive	individualist, aggressive	natural aggression	no	no	understanding of aggressive instincts	nothing clear (law and order?)

TABLE III. (continued)
Models of Human Nature

	Basic Nature	Social Inclination	Flaw	Remarkability	Freedom to Choose	Salvation	Social Action Propensity
Cultural* (Geertz, Arendt, Campbell)	ambiguous	social (with a vengeance)	strains between culture and structure (Hunting—Washburn)	maybe	up to a point	knowledge and action	welfare state
Catholic	on balance more good than bad	naturally social, organic	finitude, fear, birth in sinful race	no, save by long organic growth	yes, but often no	growth in charity, restoration, reconstruction, reconciliation	subsidiarity, localism, "natural" groups

* A widespread combination of these three models is, or has been, the more or less conventional wisdom of America's cultural elites. Call it "liberal humanism." It also includes elements—not always consistent—of other models, e.g., socialism, neo-Freudianism, behaviorism, and more recently even ethology. It now seems to be in retreat.

to create new social structures to resocialize human nature; simply get rid of the whole superstructure of technological affluence in society and the basic nature of human nature will reassert itself. Indeed, from the anarchist viewpoint (as well as from the Catholic, incidentally) there is little to choose from between the vast corporate bureaucracies of state capitalism and the vast corporate bureaucracies of state socialism. The anarchist may consider himself a socialist, but he is not a Marxist, and he does not, as do Marxists outside the socialist countries, desperately rush from new-Marxist state to new-Marxist state looking for confirmation in *praxis* of the socialist theories. For the anarchist does not believe that state socialism is free from the dead weight of hyperorganized, technological affluent society. Some socialist states—Cuba and China, for example—may attract the anarchist because they do seem to show some propensity to decentralize decision-making, if the articles he reads in his newspapers and magazines are to be believed. However, having been burned before by Marxist socialist societies, the anarchist is much less likely than his Marxist counterpart to proclaim enthusiastically, "I have seen the future and it works!"

It is understandable, however, that the Marxist-socialist desperately looks for social experiments that will confirm his faith, for by his own definition (and by his Marxist theory) the ultimate validation of the Marxist model is to be found in *praxis*. Human nature will indeed be made when it is freed from the chains of capitalist oppression. "If only," the socialist will say, "we can find a society which did that, then we would have all the evidence we need." Hence the grand pilgrimages of socialists to Cuba and China, and hence, too, the Frankfurter school* of sociology in Germany, which is Marxist and

---

*For the Frankfurter school, sociological hypotheses deal with the way society *ought* to be organized in a Marxist system. When control of the means of production is in the hands of the workers, a healthy society—devoid of the weaknesses of contemporary society—will emerge. Hypotheses are confirmed not by the collection of empirical data—as is typical of American sociology—but by *orthopraxis*, a testing against the realities of an authentic socialist society. One of the advantages of the theories of the Frankfurter school is that they don't need any evidence to write about them.

socialist but also extremely critical of all existing socialist states. The confirmation of its hypotheses, the Frankfurter school contends, will not come from empirical evidence but only from the *praxis* of an authentic socialist society. Unfortunately, by the criteria set up by them, there is no such thing as an authentic Marxist society and there probably never will be.

Behaviorism is much more modest in setting out its model of human nature. It does not want to change humankind, only to modify its conditioning. As far as enhancing freedom and dignity, it thinks that people ought to be conditioned so that they realize that such concepts are in effect "category mistakes" (Behaviorist terminology for inaccurate use of language). People are bad because they have received bad reinforcements; they will be good if they receive good reinforcements. In either case, you don't have to worry about abstract metaphysical speculation about whether human nature is good or bad and about what constitutes humankind's basic flaw. Most social scientists are appalled by the Skinnerian synthesisms; however, it would be a mistake to underestimate how congenial behaviorism is to biological and physiological scientists who are concerned about human behavior. To them, Skinner makes a good deal of sense.

Neo-Freudianism, socialism, and behaviorism are on the left of the contemporary semi-Pelagian responses about human nature. They are the radical positions. On the right, inside the neo-Pelagian camp, are the classical liberalism of Rousseau and, in some sense, of Thomas Jefferson and the romanticism of Stendhal, Nietzsche, and more recently, Norman O. Brown. It would be no exaggeration to say that the vast majority of ordinary American citizens have a political ideology that is a mixture in varying amounts of classical liberalism and romanticism. It is ignorance and tyranny that make humans bad, says the classical liberal, and knowledge and freedom that will enable him to be virtuous. There was a time when such "Lockean" optimism did not seem naïve; however, in the 1970s, the classical liberal faith is certainly under severe strain.

The romantic sees the basic human flaw to be excessive rationality and believes that salvation is achievable through the release of sentiments and feelings, or the unleashing of, in Brown's words, the "polymorphous perversity" of the id. Politics are much less important for the romantic than they are for the other contemporary semi-Pelagians. Salvation is indeed social, because, like the anarchists and unlike the other semi-Pelagians, the romantics defend the basic human nature even in its present form. However, the romantic's social inclination is almost always dyadic, and the romantic posture toward the rest of the world tends to be egoism *à deux*. Hence the social propensities of romanticism emphasize sensibility, emotionality, and withdrawal from the ugly complexities of the world into romantic love. When one engages in politics at all, it is not the politics of elections or even the politics of social reform but rather the politics of gesture, the politics of liturgy (made popular by the brothers Berrigan). When one mixes romanticism with anarchism (and the undisciplined romanticism of Roszak and not the disciplined romanticism of the Proudhonites), one has a blend that appeals strongly to the counterculture and the New Left. This blend may call itself socialist, but it is certainly not Marxian in its origins and would be severely repressed in any Marxist socialist society.

All the contemporary semi-Pelagians believe in the possibility of salvation. Personal authenticity, maturity, liberation, the end of society as we know it, better conditioning, knowledge and freedom, the release of sentiment and polymorphous perversity—all are possible, indeed all could be easy in some fundamental sense. Hence the anger—sometimes verging on paranoia—of many semi-Pelagians. Humankind *ought* to be better than it is. The tyranny of dependency relationships or economic structures or ignorance of technology or the affluent society or bad conditioning is simply intolerable; and "they" who are responsible for such tyranny are evil not only because they do evil but because their oppression is forcing others to do evil. All humans of good faith and intelligence, honesty and moral virtue must unite against "them."

It hardly need be said that the various models of human nature in Table III are not mutually exclusive; they are rather abstractions pulled out of contemporary life. In the personal ideologies of many people, these various models can be blended and combined—not perhaps without contradiction and inconsistency, but still when one is at the level of symbols and unselfconscious pictures, inconsistency is not often a problem. I suspect it would not be difficult to find a good many Americans, particularly those on the staffs of the nation's higher educational institutions, who combine symbols from the Freudian, socialist, anarchist, Behaviorist, liberal, and romantic systems into their own highly eclectic, but nonetheless personally satisfying, preconscious ideologies. Indeed, there is nothing to prevent them from going across to the Manichaean side to add neo-Manichaean and ethological pictures to their repertoire.

All the models of human nature on the top of Table III believe in salvation whether easy or arduous to attain. But once one comes to the lower half of the table, one encounters a much more grim and pessimistic view of the future—a view that is rapidly becoming dominant in America's high culture. Such neo-Manichaeans as Robert Heilbroner, Richard Goodwin, Loren Eiseley, and the ecological and environmental apocalyptic preachers literally dominate the bastions of high culture just now. They are strongly reinforced by the popularity of the literature on human aggressiveness, whether it be done by professional ethologists as Konrad Lorenz, rather dubious anthropologists as Lionel Tiger, or popularizers as Robert Ardrey. Human nature is fundamentally evil, and the individualist, egoist, aggressive, self-seeking behavior we view in the society around us is not the result of bad conditioning or bad social structures or bad socialization; rather it is fundamental to the human condition, the result, as Loren Eiseley put it, of a major and ultimately self-destructive mistake in the evolutionary process made three million years ago. The Manichaeans take a dim view of things, to put the matter mildly. Loren Eiseley tells us:

It is with the coming of man that a vast hole seems to open in nature, a vast black whirlpool spinning faster and faster, consuming flesh, stones, soil, minerals, sucking down the lightning, wrenching power from the atom, until the ancient sounds of nature are drowned in the cacophony of something which is no longer nature, something instead which is loose and knocking at the world's heart, something demonic and no longer planned—escaped, it may be—spewed out of nature, contending in a final giant's game against its master.[6]

William C. Pollard comments on Eiseley's prophecy of doom and makes clear the nature of the problem for humankind when he tells us that any planet that produces thinking creatures is courting catastrophe:

> Reserves of fossil fuel laid down over a span of 100 million years, especially of petroleum and natural gas, are being rapidly exhausted. Spills pollute the surface of the ocean, and in burning these fuels the Earth's atmosphere is being polluted and its carbon dioxide is steadily rising. The lakes and rivers that so recently graced the Earth are being made unfit for either man or fish. The wilderness is shrinking and being converted into either vast urban sprawls or junk heaps. Many strange and wonderful species of living things have already become extinct since man appeared, and many hundreds more rapidly approaching extinction. All other living things are finding life more and more difficult in the face of man. Perhaps it is true that any planet anywhere in the universe that acquires a noosphere is courting catastrophe.[7]

But still one must be careful of the Manichaean argument. Their logic compels them to predict apocalypse. Human nature is bad and unreformable, and that is that. Heilbroner at least is clear-eyed enough and intellectually honest enough to acknowledge the fact that one rallies around the great god Atlas to pick up the burdens of the world not with any hope of salvation but to wait bravely for the end. Yet many Manichaeans are still Protestants with the fundamentalist fervor of Protestant preachers; they are still liberals in the classic sense of the word, still products of two thousand years of Western culture. Scratch a neo-Manichaean and you may find a neo-Pelagian. Salvation may still be possible, though it has now become extremely difficult. We must all be terrified, we must all work hard, we must all make immense sacrifices, we must all be ready to turn our fate over to the neo-Manichaeans, but it is just possible that salvation can be obtained. Thus Pollard adds to his vision of apocalypse a faint glimmer of hope:

> The problem that confronts us most urgently is whether mankind throughout the world can change sufficiently radically in time to convert the present curse into a blessing. My own view is that he will not do so until he has suffered greatly and much that he now relies upon has been destroyed. As the Earth in a short few decades becomes twice as crowded with human beings as it is now, and as human societies are confronted with dwindling resources in the midst of mounting accumulations of wastes and a steadily deteriorating environment, we can only foresee social paroxysms of an intensity greater than any we have so far known. The problems are so varied and so vast and the means for their solution so far beyond the resources of the scientific and technological know-how on which we have relied that there simply is not time to avoid the impending catastrophe. We stand, therefore, on the threshold of a time of judgment more severe, undoubtedly, than any that mankind has ever faced before in history.[8]

So it is not the end to humankind that we are anticipating but merely the end of civilization and, Pollard tells us, the beginning of postcivilization, something that we cannot even begin to imagine but that may in fact turn out to be paradisal. And Eiseley, who always seems to me to be the most arrogant and angry of the Manichaeans, seems to think the possibility of salvation exists for nature if not for humankind:

> It may be we who go. I am just primitive enough to hope that somehow, somewhere, a cardinal may still be whistling on a green bush when the last man goes blind before his man-made sun. If it should turn out that we have mishandled our lives as several civilizations before us have done, it seems a pity that we should involve the violet and the tree frog in our departure. To perpetrate this final act of malice seems somehow disproportionate beyond endurance. It is like tampering with the secret purposes of the universe itself and involving not just man but life in the final holocaust—an act of petulant, deliberate blasphemy.[9]

If the process is inevitable, if it is all the result of the basic flaw that was introduced into the evolutionary process when rationality emerged, then why are Eiseley and Pollard and their ilk so angry? If, on the other hand, there is some hope, then the introduction of rationality was not a fatal flaw after all. The neo-Manichaeans' heritage inclines them to believe in salvation, which their anger and hope support, but their prophetic visions deny the possibility; and so they are caught, suspended between hope and despair, salvation and doom.

There are other, less manic versions of semi-Manichaeanism. The capitalist view of man, for example, rather benignly thinks that the competition of the marketplace turns the aggressive self-seeking of individuals into a benign and balanced common good. Konrad Lorenz may rage about civilized man's eight deadly sins, but he still believes that overpopulation, devastation of the environment, genetic decay, etc., can be reversed, particularly if we understand the nature of human aggressiveness. After all, Lorenz points out, humans are one of the few species that kill conspecifics (perhaps because they have rather limited abilities at recognizing others as being from the same species, i.e., as being "human as we are").

Frequently confused with the capitalist model of human nature is the classic conservative model. It is given its most famous expression by Edmund Burke and reechoed in very different terms today by the Trillings and, more recently, by some of the "new Tories," most notably, Irving Kristol, Daniel Bell, and Nathan Glazer. Such writers are deeply impressed by the difficulty of maintaining a social order. Bell, in his *The Cultural Contradictions of Capitalism*, cites with sympathy Joseph Conrad's protest against Friedrich Nietzsche's romanticism: "civilization is a thin coating of protection against the anarchic impulses and atavistic roots of life which lurk just below the surface of existence and which constantly press to burst out. For Nietzsche, it is the will to power which is the road to salvation; for Conrad, it is the will to power which threatens civilization."[10]

Human nature is flawed by pride and irrationality, by its anarchistic impulses. It is, perhaps, weakly cooperative but hardly capable of being remade. Social policy must seek to maintain order and stability because, if they are lost, all else is lost. Many of the new Tories were originally Marxists, Trotskyists, or liberals; however, they were also faithful students of the Trillings, who maintained a firm defense of pessimism during the 1930s, 1940s, and 1950s against the tide of socialist or liberal optimism that swirled around Columbia University. Hence, when the (in retrospect, relatively minor) political and social disruptions of the 1960s emerged, the new Tories found themselves frightened by the possibility that the Trillings might have been right after all. They very quickly began to preach about the importance of the social order and "civility." However, it does not follow that the new Tories are necessarily political conservatives, though they have become philosophical conservatives. It is quite possible to take a Burkean position and still support social policies oriented toward change and reform. Nathan Glazer continues to do so, as does Daniel P. Moynihan, who is not, I think, a Burkean conservative, although he is closely linked in many respects to the new Tories. (Moynihan is by temperament and disposition, if not by articulated position, a Catholic; and the guaranteed annual income, his major contribution to American social-policy recommendations, comes right out of the Catholic social theory position.) But even if one supports liberal political programs, one does so from a perspective that is both ambivalent and gradualist.*

Though Reinhold Niebuhr does not distinguish sharply between the kingdom of God and the kingdom of man, the kingdom of love and the kingdom of justice, his views on the nature of human nature are still a classic statement of the Protestant position. They ought to be read if only for the strong evidence they present that even a very up-to-date and modern Protestant scholar was fundamentally grim and pessimistic

---

* Not part of the Columbia-Harvard group but still a militant new Tory philosophically is Prof. Edward Shils of the Committee of Social Thought, of the University of Chicago. Shils, however, having signed the petition of Professors for Nixon, has now apparently become a political conservative. There is some irony in seeing such a vigorous critic of Joseph McCarthy putting his name on an advertisement sponsored by The Committee to Reelect the President (CREEP) in his old age.

about humankind. Luther, even Manes, could not have been more specific:

> Man is insecure and involved in natural contingency; he seeks to overcome his insecurity by a will-to-power which over-reaches the limits of human creatureliness. Man is ignorant and involved in the limitations of a finite mind; but he pretends that he is not limited. He assumes that he can gradually transcend finite limitations until his mind becomes identical with universal mind. All of his intellectual and cultural pursuits, therefore, become infected with the sin of pride. Man's pride and will-to-power disturb the harmony of creation. The Bible defines sin in both religious and moral terms. The religious dimension of sin is man's rebellion against God, his effort to usurp the place of God. The moral and social dimension of sin is injustice. The ego which falsely makes itself the centre of existence in its pride and will-to-power inevitably subordinates other life to its will and thus does injustice to other life.[11]

It is not merely a matter of a minor human flaw; rather it is something that pertains to the very nature of human nature. Man is always and everywhere evil. Pride and sensuality are the twin attempts to escape from his own finite anxieties, but they are doomed to failure:

> Man knows more than the immediate natural situation in which he stands and he constantly seeks to understand his immediate situation in terms of a total situation. Yet he is unable to define the total human situation without colouring his definition with finite perspectives drawn from his immediate situation. The realization of the relativity of his knowledge subjects him to the peril of scepticism. The abyss of meaninglessness yawns on the brink of all his mighty spiritual endeavours. Therefore man is tempted to deny the limited character of his knowledge, and the finiteness of his perspectives. He pretends to have achieved a degree of knowledge which is beyond the limit of finite life. This is the "ideological taint" in which all human knowledge is involved and which is always something more than mere human ignorance. It is always partly an effort to hide that ignorance by pretension.[12]

Niebuhr had an immense influence on social policy-makers and social activists in the 1930s, 1940s, and 1950s. I am tempted to say that his influence was strong despite his views about human nature; for most of the activists of those three decades were optimistic by disposition. Still, they were enough part of the American Protestant cultural heritage to recognize a strong strain of their own latent fears about human nature. In the pessimism of Niebuhr humans are both proud and sensual:

> Anxiety about perfection and about insecurity are thus inexorably bound together in human actions and the errors which are made in the search for perfection are never due merely to the ignorance of not knowing the limits of conditioned values. They always exhibit some tendency of the agent to hide his own limits, which he knows only too well. Obviously the basic source of temptation is, therefore, not the inertia of "matter" or "nature" against the larger and the more inclusive ends which reason envisages. It resides in the inclination of man, either to deny the contingent character of his existence (in pride and self-love) or to escape from his freedom (in sensuality). Sensuality represents an effort to escape from the freedom and the infinite possibilities of spirit by becoming lost in the detailed processes, activities and interests of existence, an effort which results inevitably in unlimited devotion to limited values. Sensuality is man "turning inordinately to mutable good" (Aquinas).[13]

The grimness of the Heilbroners and the Eiseleys is only a step beyond that of Niebuhr, though the latter, because he believed human nature was being redeemed by God (without modification), could at least justify continued action by the children of light against the children of darkness, by moral man in an immoral society. If one takes away Christian faith, however, one ends up grimly contemplating the god Atlas with Robert Heilbroner.

Reinhold Niebuhr, Calvinist Protestant that he was, thought that a combination of the heedless sacrifice of the saintly and the rough justice of the law could lead to at least a tolerable society, and traditional Lutheran pessimism thought that a combination of personal belief in God's forgiveness and righteousness on the part of the ruler's "terrible swift sword" would at least make social living possible if not particularly pleasant. But the presently fashionable response to the Lutheran, Niebuhrian, Calvinist, and capitalist, moderate and restrained forms of pessimism is to say that such relatively benign (truly semi-Pelagian) positions were only tenable before Vietnam and before Watergate—or alternatively, before the Holocaust and the atomic bomb.* There is a certain naïve temporal ethnocentrism in such an attitude. The post-Watergate, post-Vietnam, post-Hiroshima, post-Dachau generations were not the first ones to discover the existence of evil in the world, nor were they the first to discover the failure of the liberal optimistic dreams of the eighteenth and nineteenth centuries. The migrants to industrial America, the child factory workers of nineteenth-century England and France, the young men who died in Flanders' fields all knew long before the tenured faculty members of the great American universities that modernization and the scientific revolution had not eliminated evil from the human condition.

The semi-Pelagian dimension of Augustine's dilemma has been dominant since the time of Voltaire, but the semi-Manichaean dimension has never been eliminated, and at least in orthodox Protestant theory, it remains strong and vigorous. In the United States, the product of a peculiar liaison between Puritan Protestantism and Enlightenment deism, two views of the nature of human nature have been locked in combat since the beginning. The present shift of the balance in the Manichaean direction may be nothing more than another swing of the pendulum. However, contemporary Manichaeanism of the Heilbroner-Eiseley variety is certainly vigorous. I wonder if ever in the history of the republic optimism about human nature has ever been so unpopular.

In addition to the Manichaeans and the Pelagians of our time, there are two positions that try to hedge their bets—a position I call the "cultural" model of man, which commands

---

* A Catholic theological response would be to say that optimism is only tenable before the death of a single child, and that six million deaths should not make the problem qualitatively different. One death is intolerable.

the allegiance of most sociologists and anthropologists who bother to think seriously about such matters, and the Catholic position. The Parsons school is certainly committed to such a perspective, and if I choose Clifford Geertz to exemplify it (particularly in his *The Interpretation of Cultures*), it is because I find him much easier to understand than Parsons. Also Hannah Arendt seems to use a similar model, as does Edward Shils in his own supercilious fashion and, much more specifically but more clearly, Gerald Suttles, especially in his critiques of the "territorialists" such as Robert Ardrey.

Those who are committed to the cultural model shy away from explicit discussion of the basic nature of human nature (it is difficult to imagine Clifford Geertz, for example, making an undisciplined comment like Pollard's about a planet producing a noosphere at the risk of its own self-destruction). Human nature is surely social in this model; indeed, as Geertz points out, it is social before it is human. Conflict occurs largely because human cultural capabilities do not develop quite so rapidly as the human social structures. Our moral, ethical, and political skills lag behind the institutions that our ingenuity has produced. Physical anthropologist Sherwood Washburn can go so far as to suggest that original sin was the shift from a food-gathering to a hunting society. Humankind sinned by becoming carnivorous, and since then our moral development has not been able to keep up with our technological skills. But salvation, Hannah Arendt tells us, is still possible through knowledge and action. We cannot remake ourselves totally, perhaps, but at least some modifications can occur, and we have some freedom. The welfare state, or welfare-state socialism, seems to those who are committed, however ambiguously, to a cultural model to be the only way that knowledge and action can be translated into political and social policy—though one has only moderate hopes for the success of such policies.

An interesting variant of the cultural model has been advanced recently in a very sophisticated presidential address to the American Psychological Association by Donald T. Campbell.[14] Campbell notes the persuasive argument that natural biological selection would produce an ever more aggressive and destructive evolutionary type and suggests that human culture—the product of social evolution—develops altruistic norms to hold this biological destructiveness in check. The religious and moral codes of ancient urban civilizations, he comments, have much in common wherever they appear in the world, precisely because they represent the social wisdom that had evolved as a precondition for the development of complex urban life. Social evolution, in other words, counters the individual selfish tendencies that biological evolution has tended to select as a result of the genetic competition among the co-operators.

Humankind's tendency to evil, in other words, results from the fierce competition of the survival-of-the-fittest evolutionary process. Humankind's tendency to good results from the evolution of a value system that checks the aggressive tendencies of the personality and makes cooperation—necessary for species survival—possible. The war between good and evil in the self is the war between biological evolution and social evolution.

Campbell is thus in the excellent strategic position of conceding to the sociobiologists (a group of scholars profoundly pessimistic about human nature—E. O. Wilson, M. T. Ghiselin, R. D. Alexander) that a genetically more aggressive variety of humanity may have evolved and at the same time arguing that the countervailing process of social evolution is producing a greater level of self-sacrificing altruism that keeps the aggressiveness in check. But his conclusions are apt to be disconcerting to most psychologists (as Campbell admits): if the traditional moral and religious wisdom is the result of social evolution, then it must be treated with a good deal more respect than psychologists normally treat it. Recognition of the reality of sin and the importance of repressing certain vices may be socially functional even though psychology is reluctant to admit it.

Campbell is by his own admission a hard-nosed "reductionist" psychologist, so his arguments against the psychologists' contempt for religious and moral inhibitions takes on a special force:

I am indeed asserting a social functionality and psychological validity to concepts such as temptation and original sin due to human carnal, animal nature.

For the social system to work best, the participants in it should have behavioral dispositions optimizing social system purposes rather than individual purposes, where these differ.

Committing oneself to living for a transcendent Good's purposes, not one's own, is a commitment to optimize the social system rather than the individual system. Social groups effectively indoctrinating such individual commitments might well have had a social-evolutionary advantage and thus have discovered a functional adaptive truth.

Religious beliefs leading a person to optimize behavior over a longer time perspective than one's own life, especially beliefs in afterlife with compensatory rewards for deprivations in this life, would also further social system functioning and would also reflect a fundamental social truth.[15]

Campbell's reflections, if they are taken seriously by the profession, will mark a profound revolution in psychological thinking. Campbell, beginning from his own reductionist position, has ended up with a model of human nature that in its own context is remarkably like that of Thomas Aquinas. Humankind is a mixture of good and evil, with the good slightly more powerful than the evil because of the need for goodness to sustain human cooperation. Altruism plays the same role in Campbell's model that charity plays in Aquinas'.

As was noted earlier in this chapter, eclecticism is not only possible in one's ideological symbols but easy. One can readily mix the cultural model with the liberal and Niebuhrian models, as well as some images from socialism, Freudianism, behaviorism, and romanticism. The result is a blend of images and pictures that in varying proportion provide the personal symbol system of much of the American elite that I will call, for lack of a better name, liberal humanism. This system (perhaps because of its formal agnostic stance on religion) likes to shy away from basic questions. It is reluctant to address itself specifically to what it believes to be the nature of human nature; hence, it is relatively easy to combine in the same system of pictures relatively optimistic and relatively pessimistic imagery. However, this refusal to face basic questions gives an individual a great deal of flexibility in arranging and rearranging the imagery of his own personal ideology. Liberal humanism, then, is less an ideology than it is a label under which a wide variety of highly personalized pictures and blends can be subsumed.

A Thomistic scholar like David Tracy would be horrified at my conclusion that the Catholic model of the nature of human nature is in fact the hedging of a bet, when it stands between the poles of optimism and pessimism. He would argue, I suspect, that I am conceding far too much to the dialectical, contradictory "style of religious reflection" of Protestantism. There is no reason, I think he would say, why one has to approach the phenomenon of human nature from the frame of reference of opposing polarities. The non-Western world would not understand such a *via negativa*, and the Catholic (or Thomistic) style of analogic rather than dialectical reflection provides an alternative even within the Western heritage.* Doubtless Tracy is right in this respect, as in most others. Thomistic Augustinianism as distinct from Lutheran Augustinianism can approach the Manichaean-Pelagian dilemma from the point of view of reconciling opposites instead of polarizing them. However, it will be a long time before the intellectual and rhetorical style of American culture permits one to approach the question of the nature of human nature with easy Thomistic confidence and assert, "The question is not whether human nature is evil or good; the question is rather how to explain why it is simultaneously evil *and* good." In fact, of course, that is the Catholic way.

This book is not the proper place to discuss at great length the history of the Catholic doctrine of original sin.[16] Briefly, every man, the Catholic believes, comes into the world noble and at the same time wretched, rich in a magnificent future

---

* Tracy would argue, if I understand him correctly, that the analogic style can subsume or contain within it the dialectical style. For how this can be, I urge the reader to consult Tracy's forthcoming book.

and yet inclined to evil. The ultimate root of the evil, perhaps, is to be found by our finite being. We are a limited creature with a hunger for the infinite, a mortal being, which alone of all mortal beings, is able to reflect on its own mortality. By our very nature we come into the world prepared to be afraid. In fact, we become afraid quickly and strike back to defend ourselves against those who cause us to fear. Furthermore, we are born into a sinful human condition, that is to say, we inherit the negative impact of countless generations of fear, suspicion, and distrust of the human race. We are cut off from one another not merely by our own finitude and our own acts of fear and distrust but also by all the fear, suspicion, distrust, and hatred that have become part of the human inheritance. However, we are capable of transcending our limitations, our fears, and the results of our evil heritage. The purpose of the coming of Jesus was to reinforce and to strengthen the positive, constructive, reconciling, restoring aspects of our personalities so that we could, at least up to a point, overcome both our personal fear and the hateful heritage into which we are born. It is possible, then, to grow in charity, restoration, reconciliation, reconstruction; but only after we have made an act of faith in the ultimate trustworthiness of the universe, a trustworthiness that is revealed to us by Jesus (though modern Catholic thinkers would acknowledge that the fundamental trustworthiness of the universe can be known naturally and also is preached by other thinkers besides Jesus). Nonetheless, this trustworthiness is neither self-evident nor easy to credit. When one, in other words, makes a fundamental commitment to the ultimate benignity and graciousness of both the cosmos and human life—despite considerable and persuasive evidence to the contrary—then, and only then, is one able to trust, to reconcile, to reconstruct, to restore. If one does not make such a commitment to graciousness, at least implicitly, one simply doesn't have the kind of courage to act against fears, suspicion, and hatred, and to commit oneself in the direction one's constructive, naturally social and organically linked personality would incline one to go. *In this sense*, faith is necessary to transcend (though not to eliminate) the constraints of human fear, suspicion, and hatred. Quite simply, in the Catholic world view, the basic flaw in human nature is hatred—personal and hereditary—and the hatred is overcome only by *charity*, and *charity* is only possible when one is convinced that one lives in a world sufficiently trustworthy to risk it.

The root disposition—not yet the flaw—from which evil comes is to be found not in the fact that humankind is a composite of body and soul, but rather in the fact that humankind is finite—like every creature—and knows its finitude— unlike any other creature. Because we are mortal and are capable of reflecting on our mortality, we are also capable of fear (like other bodily creatures); but we are also capable of distrust, a uniquely human characteristic.

The sin of the human race is the sin of distrust—of cosmic distrust; it is the sin of refusing to believe that the universe in which we find ourselves is trustworthy and therefore the sin of refusing to believe that the power that produced the universe and placed us in it is trustworthy. Since we cannot trust the cosmos or its creator, we cannot trust anyone but ourselves and hence are driven to put our security and our confidence solely in our own powers and abilities. Thus, we cannot take even the risk of treating other humans as trustworthy.

Refusing to believe in the trustworthiness of others is called hatred. Making an act of faith in the trustworthiness of others is called love. The sin of the race, therefore, is the sin of hatred. We commit our own personal sins of hatred, but we are also born into a sinful race that has accumulated predispositions to hatred and the results of hatred down through the generations. The blend of our own predisposition to distrust and the accumulated distrust of the centuries is what constitutes the evil in us. But there is also the contrary and very powerful predisposition toward trusting union with others— our nature as social beings thrusts us powerfully in that direction. Thus the human personality is the arena in which conflicting forces of trust and distrust, love and hatred, fear and faith conflict. The Catholic Christian believes that there is more good than evil in human nature, more cooperation than selfishness, more trust than distrust, more love than hatred— though sometimes just barely. It believes that in the human personality there is the capacity for reconciliation, reconstruction, restoration. Because of personal and hereditary limitations we can exercise this capacity only imperfectly, but such an exercise is by no means impossible. However, we can only engage in sustained love and reconciliation when we have first made an act of faith in the fundamental trustworthiness of the universe. In this sense, faith in God is essential to overcome the sinful dispositions of our personality and our race. Jesus came to reveal to us in a superabundance how loving is the fundamental power of the universe and, hence, how worthy of receiving our trust. Jesus came to tell us that we need not fear, that we could take the risk of vulnerability required by loving reconciliation. Thus it is in and through Jesus as the revelation of the loving trustworthiness of God (and the cosmos and life he has created) that we overcome the effects of the sin of the human race. The Catholic Christian today acknowledges, of course, that there are other ways of learning of God's loving trustworthiness than through Jesus. The Lord, however, is the way par excellence. The Catholic Christian also notes, however, that many who do not know Jesus—and alas some who do—neither believe in the trustworthiness of life nor act as if they thought it was safe to risk oneself in love.

Love for the Catholic Christian is not so much the desire to possess someone else as the desire to be possessed by the other. Love is the passionate and devout commitment of one person to the welfare and happiness of another. In such a commitment, the personal identity of the first person is not lost but enhanced because the most noble and most generous aspects of his personality are called forth. To possess another in love does not mean to be possessive of him. It means, rather, to graciously accept his passionate and devout commitment to my welfare and happiness, to assume that there is a tendency toward permanence in that commitment, and at the same time, to respect the radical freedom of the other. It is a risk to expose onself to the vulnerability of such a commitment—for the other may come to reject our passionate and devout commitment. It is an equal risk to accept such a commitment (and give it in return) because respect for the radical freedom of the other leaves one open to the possibility of a devastating exercise by the other of that freedom.

We must even respect the freedom of God, though we know that He has permanently and implacably committed himself to love for us. The permanence of that commitment—like the permanence of any human commitment—is found in the freedom of God and not in any "legal" or economic claim ("possessiveness") we might wish to have on him.

The "paradise" that was "lost" by human sin is a relationship between humankind and God in which, despite our mortal, creaturely, and human propensity to fear and distrust, humans still stood in a relationship with God in which they accepted Him as trustworthy and gave themselves to Him in love and, through Him, gave themselves to one another. Whether and how such a historic paradise may have existed, however, is not the point of Christian revelation, which is concerned with the restoration of human faith in God's loving trustworthiness, through his self-revelation in Jesus—and in particular, in the death and resurrection of Jesus. (Some Catholic writers suggest that the paradise story looks both to the past events and also to the present and future opportunities God, particularly through His self-disclosure in Jesus, offers humankind for reconciliation and unity—both individual and collective. These are opportunities that humankind repeatedly rejects but that God repeatedly offers again.) Such a restoration re-creates the situation as it should be, whether or not it had ever in fact existed in the past. Reconciliation in love and trust is a fundamental longing of humankind and the basic aspiration of human nature—even if our finitude and our resulting fear and distrust impede our efforts toward such a goal. The underlying flaw in human nature, its basic and tragic weakness, its essential deprivation is that its propensity to suspicion and distrust conflicts with its propensity to openness and trust. Its self-defending hatred conflicts with its self-giving love.*

* The above summary of the Catholic position is both simplified and demythologized, and deliberately avoids a number of issues that have preoccupied theologians for a long time—issues that are not especially relevant to our present context and may not, indeed, be relevant to any important context in the contemporary world. However, the reader, Catholic or non-Catholic, may rest assured that this summary has been shown to the appropriate Catholic theologians who do indeed pronounce it as an accurate summary of their present thinking. It is also a reflection

It must be stressed that this Catholic view of the fundamental human flaw is categorically and systematically different from the Protestant view. Many non-Catholics are quite unaware of the difference, perhaps because the rather rigid devotional forms of Catholicism that they encounter in their daily lives seem to assume a human perversity as great as that assumed by even the most pessimistic Protestants. However, Niebuhr was under no illusions about the difference between his Calvinistic pessimism and what seemed to him to be Catholic optimism. He dismissed Catholicism as semi-Pelagian, because, as far as he could see, the Catholic doctrine of the nature of human nature was quite indistinguishable from that of Pelagius:

> The official Catholic doctrine of original sin, usually regarded as "Semi-Pelagian," does not greatly vary the emphasis of Pelagianism. The doctrine presupposes a distinction between the *pure naturalia*, the essential character of man as man and a "further gift" (*donum superadditum*) which God bestowed upon man in addition to his natural creation. This distinction, first suggested by Athanasius and achieving its final definition in the system of Aquinas, enables Catholic theology to incorporate the Biblical idea of the Fall without disturbing the concept of original sin as an inertia of nature. For in the Fall, the *donum superadditum* is lost and, until restored by sacramental grace, man is subject to the natural limitations of his finite nature. Original sin is thus described negatively. It is the privation of something that does not belong to man essentially and, therefore, cannot be regarded as a corruption of his essential nature. As in Pelagianism a basic purpose of the doctrine is to guard against conceptions of total depravity which destroy the idea of responsibility and thereby vitiate the very meaning of sin. The logical difficulties of the Augustinian doctrine are thus avoided, and the peril of denying the structure of freedom in the assertion of its corruption is averted, as in Pelagianism. But the question remains whether

---

of the ancient Catholic tradition that is to be found even in Augustine, who was, for example, much more concerned about the "collective Adam," the whole of humankind, than he was about the individual Adam.

either Pelagianism or Semi-Pelagianism is true to the psychological and moral facts in human wrong-doing.[17]

One can disagree that the position is semi-Pelagian (and most Catholic theologians would) and still agree that Niebuhr has described it accurately enough. This book is not the place to attempt to lay out once again the classic controversy of the Reformation and the Counter Reformation. The Catholic position would agree with Niebuhr that man is insecure, ignorant, anxious; and that anxiety is the internal precondition of sin. But it would insist that such ignorance, insecurity, and anxiety is natural in any finite creature able to reflect upon its own finitude, any mortal creature able to reflect on its own mortality. But such a flaw does not make human nature depraved, even though it may give it a hell of a lot of problems.

It is not my purpose in this volume to argue that the Catholic view of the nature of human nature is the correct one, though clearly I believe that it is. Nor do I wish to insist that, correct or not, it is by far the most attractive model, one of which even the most skeptical and agnostic reader would say, "It's probably not true, but I sure as hell wish it were." In the present context, all I wish to do is to establish that such a dynamic view of the interaction between good and evil, love and hatred, faith and fear, in the human personality is the basic assumption about the nature of human nature to which the Catholic tradition is committed (though it might not always choose the language I have chosen). Such a picture, it hardly needs to be observed, will lead those who are committed to it to take a rather different perspective on human society compared to the perspective taken by those who do not have such imagery in their preconscious.

One may argue, though with some difficulty, about the modernization phenomenon (because ultimately it is a testable hypothesis), but it is virtually impossible to argue about the human-nature vector, for such a vector results from imagery so primal and so fundamental and is concerned with phenomena so variegated and unpredictable that argumentation is ultimately absurd. One chooses one's position pretty much as a matter of existential faith; I lay out the various alternatives in

Table III for the sake of clarity, with little thought of argumentation or persuasion.

Yet if I may be permitted one small and perhaps not altogether ecumenical jab: the Catholic model is not unlike the model toward which social-science theorists as Geertz and Arendt and Suttles are tentatively probing with the data and the theories of their disciplines. The difference between the Catholic model and their own as yet not fully sketched-out model, it seems to me, is that they are not as confident as are Catholic theorists in the ultimate trustworthiness of the universe. Both the cultural theorists and Catholic theorists would agree about the ambiguity of the data: the Catholic theorist has made the leap beyond it; the cultural theorist, wherever he may stand in his own personal life, has yet to do so in his theoretical articulation.

In Table IV, I have reduced to the artificial and oversimplified schematization of a two-by-two table, a matrix set up by the intersection of the human-nature and modernization vectors. Socialism and capitalism, I would submit, are both committed to modernization as description and prescription. Anarchism and classical Christianity (whether Catholic or Lutheran) reject modernization as a norm (and Catholicism also rejects it as a description). Socialism and anarchism believe in the rather quick remakability of human nature, while capitalism and Christianity are much less sanguine on the matter. However, Catholic Christianity, while not believing in easy and quick remakability, does believe that human nature is capable of organic growth in its network of social relationships and that society is therefore capable of reconstruction and reconciliation. Hence Catholicism is not as high as anarchism and socialism on the question of remakability vector and is not as low on that vector as either capitalism or classical Lutheranism. I have placed liberal humanism on the positive side of the modernization vector but have it straddling the remakability of human-nature vector, since at various times in its history in the United States, liberal humanism has tended in one direction or the other and still tries to combine positive and negative imagery about the nature of human nature.

I could add other ideologies to the matrix. Thus the neo-

TABLE IV.
A Matrix for Current Ideologies

MODERNIZATION

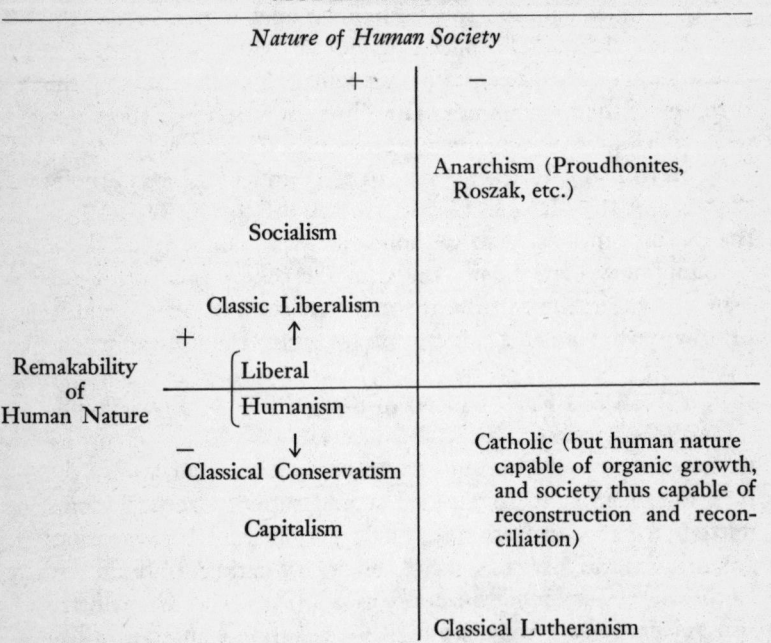

Nature of Human Society

	+	−
		Anarchism (Proudhonites, Roszak, etc.)
	Socialism	
	Classic Liberalism	
+	↑	
Remakability	⌠Liberal	
of	⌡Humanism	
Human Nature		
−	↓	Catholic (but human nature
	Classical Conservatism	capable of organic growth,
		and society thus capable of
	Capitalism	reconstruction and recon-
		ciliation)
		Classical Lutheranism

Manichaeans would be placed on the far-right-hand side of the page in their rejection of modernization and also toward the very bottom of the page in their pessimism about the remakability of human nature. However, there are only four systematically thought-out political and social ideologies in competition in the North Atlantic world at the present time: capitalism and socialism dominate the discussion, Catholicism and anarchism demand with various degrees of vigor and persistence to be admitted to the dialogue. In the next chapter I will compare the Catholic ideology with the capitalist and socialist ideology, noting in passing the differences and similarities between Catholicism and anarchism.

CHAPTER 5

୧ ୧ ୧

Capitalist, Socialist, and Anarchist Ideologies

"THE emerging consensus," said my friend who works in a private organization concerned with international economic problems, "is that food aid is at best only a short-run solution. Over the long haul, the LDC's [lesser developed countries] are going to have to acquire the capability of producing most of their own food. Only when that happens will they achieve a sufficient level of prosperity to deal with their birth-rate problem. And so there's no way of getting around it: it may not be sexy and it may be hard to see, but there's no substitute for rural development."

I wondered from my urban perspective what he meant by "rural development."

"The only solution is to improve the productivity of the peasant farmer. It turns out you don't do that by pulling him out of his village and putting him into some collective commune; and you don't do it by trying to sell him a tractor. A tractor doesn't do him much good, and it will put at least ten others out of work. What you've got to do is to find out what he needs on his few acres, listen to his problems, and help him to improve his skills, his techniques, and his work. You'll have a hard time changing his world view, so you've got to adapt your innovations to fit into his world. It may be a difficult process, but there is no peasant in the world who will resist increased productivity when he finds that it's no threat to his values or to his village."

My head whirled with a combination of vertigo and *déjà vu*. I was back in the late 1940s and early 1950s. Everyone was reading Maritain and Mounier, admiring the work of Eric Gill, and insisting that Hilaire Belloc's distributism was a viable alternative to capitalism and socialism. The National Catholic Rural Life Conference was proclaiming salvation through the family farm; and the Baroness de Hueck and *The Grail* were proclaiming the survival of Christian community. Here, within a stone's throw of the Brookings Institute, I was hearing the very same line.

Consider:

> If the nature of change is such that nothing is left for the fathers to teach their sons, or for the sons to accept from their fathers, family life collapses. The life, work, and happiness of all societies depend on certain "psychological structures" which are infinitely precious and highly vulnerable. Social cohesion, cooperation, mutual respect, and above all self-respect, courage in the face of adversity, and the ability to bear hardship—all this and much else disintegrates and disappears when these "psychological structures" are gravely damaged. A man is destroyed by the inner conviction of uselessness. No amount of economic growth can compensate for such losses—though this may be an idle reflection, since economic growth is normally inhibited by them.[1]

Doesn't it sound substantially like something a Catholic personalist or distributist would have written before 1960? It is in fact taken from a book by the former chief of planning for the British Coal Board, E. F. Schumacher, published in an American edition with an introduction by, of all people, Theodore Roszak. The great wheel has swung around again, only Catholics aren't there to welcome it back. Sometime between 1955 and 1970, the Catholic social theory vanished from the scene, and Catholics with social concerns were forced to choose between capitalism and socialism. Since the latter is by far the more fashionable of the two ideologies, most Catholics have opted for soft-core socialism and have allied themselves with revolutionary forces. Of course, most of these would-be revolutionaries are college professors, bureaucrats, or clergymen, and their revolutionary activity never goes beyond talk. They issue statements, write articles, testify at USCC (United States Catholic Conference) hearings, but they never *do* much of anything.

Those who are the legitimate heirs of the Catholic social movement sit complacently by and watch their tradition being replaced by shallow and pathetic imitations of the current radical chic, while people such as Schumacher and my friend on Massachusetts Avenue are beginning to sound like Catholics of two or three decades ago. It could boggle the mind.

There are alternatives to the two allegedly competing economic philosophies and systems of capitalism and socialism (which in fact share the same set of basic assumptions). American Catholics used to argue that there was a "third way"; we have abandoned the argument just as others have taken it up. "It is far better," said one of my non-Catholic Christian colleagues, "to oppress the people in the name of the people than to oppress them in the name of greed." To which I found myself instinctively responding, "Damn it, you shouldn't oppress the people in the name of anything." "But," he said, "how else can you amass capital for economic development?" My only response was to admit that, historically, capitalism and socialism seem to have been the only two economic systems capable of storing up capital required for economic development. "But," I insisted, "that doesn't mean there aren't other ways that it could have been done, or other ways that it could be done now." Between agribusiness and the collective farm, for example, there is an alternative. The family farm and the peasant on his plot of land are likely to be more efficient in the long run than either agribusiness or the collective farm, as responsible, reasonable, sensible international economists are now beginning to argue. I am not competent enough in economic history to be able to discuss the processes of capital formation in various countries during the last century. Surely there was massive oppression of the poor in England during the Industrial Revolution—an oppression for which even now England is paying in its self-destructive class conflict. How the oppression of the robber barons in the United States will compare to the oppression of the commissars of the Soviet Union is beyond my ability to judge, though it turned out to be a lot easier to get rid of the robber barons than the commissars.

Schumacher suggests that perhaps something can be learned from the Japanese experience where small-scale, more decentralized, more labor-using forms of organization have persisted to the present day and have contributed materially to the society's vigorous growth. Schumacher notes that in both relatively socialist India and relatively capitalist Turkey the five-year economic plans regularly show a greater volume of unemployment at the end, even when the plans appear to have been fully implemented.[2] He sees four techniques as essential to begin economic growth that need not require oppression:

> First, that workplaces have to be created in the areas where the people are living now, and not primarily in metropolitan areas into which they tend to migrate.
>
> Second, that these workplaces must be, on average, cheap enough so that they can be created in large numbers without this calling for an unattainable level of capital formation and imports.
>
> Third, that the production methods employed must be relatively simple, so that the demands for high skills are minimised, not only in the production process itself but also in matters of organisation, raw material supply, financing, marketing, and so forth.
>
> Fourth, that production should be mainly from local materials and mainly for local use.[3]

A Catholic social theory need not be reactionary, although frequently in the last two centuries it has been just that—a reaction to all those social, intellectual, political, and economic developments that could be subsumed under the two labels: Enlightenment and Industrial Revolution. Lacordaire, Chateaubriand, and Montalembert in the nineteenth century and Chesterton, Belloc, Eric Gill, and to some extent Ivan Illich, in the twentieth, have articulated the Catholic social theory in opposition to industrialization, urbanization, secularization, formalization—the basic social trends of our era. In different ways, perhaps, all these Catholic social theorists have rejected the modern world and have called for the return of a prior state of organic society. The vision of a rural, almost feudal, social order was surely understandable in the time and the places from which these writers were viewing the world scene. At that state of the proceedings, you either bought the Enlightenment–Industrial Revolution world view, lock, stock, and barrel, or you rejected it totally. Such opposition to modernization was doubtless "romantic" in that the alternative order to which they wanted to return never really existed, but it is understandable, perhaps, that in order to resist the implacable forward thrust of industrialism they rejected it totally in favor of a romantic vision of the past.

However, about 1950, the extraordinary French Catholic Emmanuel Mounier decisively broke with this romanticism, and in 1975, we need no longer do battle with the moribund Enlightenment or be threatened by the now not so confident technologues of the Industrial Revolution. It is therefore possible to subscribe to science, technology, modern means of transportation, communication, parliamentary democracy, and political liberalism and at the same time reject the view of human nature and society which provided the context in which the industrial revolution occurred.*

It is not, therefore, a question of turning the clock back, at least not anymore. Catholic social theorists need not pine for a bucolic past and thus are free to ask the much more pertinent question of what sort of structural changes a Catholic social

---

* Whether it could have occurred in another context, indeed a context shaped by the social theory we intend to outline in this book, and what such an industrial revolution would have looked like, are fascinating questions which are beyond the scope of this book and perhaps beyond the scope of any meaningful answer.

theory would invoke in a world in which modern science, transportation, and communication are a given. Liberal parliamentary democracy has become a fiction, at least outside of the North Atlantic nations. Curiously enough, Catholic social theory could easily find itself one of the few defenders of science, technology, and a liberal democracy left in the world.

A contemporary Catholic social theory need not and should not call for a return to the organic social linkages of the past, but for a recognition that those linkages persist in the present. To use the terms of Ferdinand Tönnies, the German sociologist, we do not so much call for the abandonment of *Gesellschaft* (association) so that we might return to *Gemeinschaft* (community), but rather, for the recognition that *Gemeinschaft* is alive and well and doing nicely in the midst of the *Gesellschaft* world. Or, to put the matter in the terminology of American sociologist Talcott Parsons, Catholic social theory does not recommend the abandonment of the universalistic in order to return to the particularistic so much as it points out that the particularistic has survived quite successfully in the midst of a society that claims to be universalistic. One advocates, then, not a return to the past but rather a recognition of usually ignored dimensions of the present.

I think there are seven points on which there is a fundamental agreement between capitalism and socialism but which Catholic social theory must vigorously disagree. Obviously, such an outline can be only a sketch and a greatly oversimplified one at that, but it should serve as a basis for discussion. (Table V summarizes schematically the comparisons presented here.)

1. Both capitalism and socialism assume (after Thomas Hobbes and Adam Smith) that human nature in its present form is fundamentally selfish and destructive. Capitalism assumes that this is the way humankind has been always and always will be. Yet through some marvelous disposition of nature, or providence, or someone or something, the conflict of selfish, aggressive, destructive individuals (moderated by their self-interest) can combine to produce a healthy, harmonious social unity. The socialist accepts the capitalist description of human

TABLE V.
Four Political Ideologies

	Capitalist	*Socialist*	*Catholic*	*Anarchist*
1. NATURE OF HUMAN NATURE	egoistic, selfish, and not reformable	egoistic, selfish, but reformable after liberation from oppressive structure	deprived, not depraved; more to be admired than condemned; changeable, but long organic process; more cooperative than selfish	human nature naturally good—corrupted by oppression and by the state but perfectable
2. NATURE OF SOCIETY				
a. ORIGIN	free contract to promote enlightened self-interest	same as capitalist	exists spontaneously whenever there are humans because of social nature of humankind	society is natural, human nature naturally social, society antedates humanity in evolution
b. FUNCTION	minimum constraint to maintain order and prevent chaos and destruction	maximum constraint in order to remake (or liberate) human nature and create "humane" social structures	organic and cooperative; facilitative rather than coercive, though coercion necessary at times	society functions through mutualism (free contracts among individuals and federalism (contracts and agreements among local communities)
c. SOCIETY AND STATE	distinct from society but may intervene massively, particularly for benefit of corporation ("what's good for GM . . .")	identical with society; all powers in every aspect of life	distinct from society; exists as tool of society and smaller groups	state is distinct from society; state is evil and must be destroyed; society is good

TABLE V. (*continued*)
Four Political Ideologies

	Capitalist	Socialist	Catholic	Anarchist
d. SELF	private but essentially economic	public and essentially politico-economic	private and inviolable; social and personal	freedom of the individual from all authority is the absolute human goal
3. DEVELOPMENT	scientific, rational, bureaucratic; minimum state control	scientific, rational, bureaucratic; state dominated in name of "people"	must be neither successful nor moral unless it recognizes organic and differentiated unity of the web of human relationships	economic development will be served by creating or calling forth dynamics of mutualism and federalism latent in peoples—in practice those collectives that are not controlled by state
4. MODERNIZATION	good as both description and norm	same as capitalism, but must be directed in the name of the "people"	bad as description and worse as norm	Concedes modernization as description but revolts against it as a norm; frequently calls for "return" to old ways; fundamentally antimodern. Arose as revolt against state centralism among outcasts of modernization (*lumpen-proletariat*)
5. PRESENT AND FUTURE	present economic hardship justified in terms of future abundance	present political oppression justified in terms of future freedom and abundance	"pyramids of sacrifice" are immoral	present oppression of individual for whatever goals must immediately end

TABLE V. (continued)
Four Political Ideologies

	Capitalist	Socialist	Catholic	Anarchist
6. "ARCHAIC" SOCIETIES	reactionary—must be modernized; multinationals	reactionary—must be modernized; revolution	economic progress will come only when culture and structure of existing order is respected and its organic growth facilitated	since old archaic societies are models of new world to be created, existing archaic societies must be preserved by activating mutualism and federalism
7. SIZE	bureaucratic bigness—the conglomerate, the multinational, the megaversity, HEW—all technically free of centralized state	bureaucratic bigness controlled in the name of the people by centralized state	subsidiary; small is beautiful	localism, decentralization, absolute resistance to all corporate bureaucracy; resists even own organization
8. CONFLICT	law of the marketplace save when "economy of scale" dictates otherwise	instrument of progress and liberation save when you have power	inevitable and healthy within matrix of cooperation; those who set up structure-destroying conflict are dangerous	revolutionary conflict necessary (though for many only the nonviolent is acceptable); but in anarchist society of the future, social nature of humankind will make conflict unnecessary

N.B.—Fundamentally, the anarchist world view differs from the Catholic only in number 1, where it would agree with the socialist view. In practice, however, anarchists seem to be much more suspicious of the state than Catholics. "Ecological" anarchists (Roszak) are also more likely than many Catholics (though not all, e.g., Gill, Belloc, Illich, etc.) to reject modern science and technology. Both differences may result from primary differences concerning faith in the ability of human nature (in its present form!) to cope with the political and technical tools it has created.

nature as it is, but argues that humankind doesn't have to be that way always, that if the constraints of the present economic and social class structures are destroyed, human nature can be changed.

Capitalism and socialism agree that in its present version, human nature is selfish and individualistic. Emmanuel Mounier's hostile description of individualism is by no means inaccurate:

> Individualism is a system of morals, feelings, ideas and institutions in which individuals can be organized by their mutual isolation and defence. This was the ideology and the prevailing structure of Western bourgeois society in the 18th and 19th centuries. Man in the abstract, unattached to any natural community, the sovereign lord of a liberty unlimited and undirected; turning towards others with a primary mistrust, calculation and self-vindication; institutions restricted to the assurance that these egoisms should not encroach upon one another, or to their betterment as a purely profitmaking association—such is the rule of civilization now breaking up before our eyes, one of the poorest history has known. It is the very antithesis of personalism, and its dearest enemy.[4]

Socialists would disagree that this is a description of the way things have to be, but if anyone doubts their agreement with this as a description of the way things are, he should consult Herbert Marcuse's *Portrait of One-Dimensional Man*.

2. Given such a view of human nature, one can make some immediate and obvious conclusions about human society. Social organization exists to constrain the unbridled exercise of selfish irresponsibility. The state is established by individuals acting in enlightened self-interest, knowing that only the raw power of institutional force can keep them from completely destroying one another. The state exists to impose constraints. From the capitalist viewpoint, only those constraints that are necessary to establish rules of the competitive marketplace game are tolerable. Socialists respond by saying all constraints that are required to create a situation in which human nature can be remade are required. The selfishness imposed by the

present social structure must be extirpated from the human condition. For the capitalist, society will necessarily be permanently oppressive to selfish individual freedom—though hopefully the oppression will be as little as possible. For the socialist a maximum of short-range oppression is justified on the grounds that human social structures and human nature can be so modified that at some unspecified point in the future all social constraints can be dispensed with when an unselfish, generous, cooperative human nature will have been produced. In both cases, however, the present function of society and of society's political arm, the state, is to restrain and oppress; and in both cases such restraint and oppression are to be imposed on individuals for their own good—in the one case for the continuation of the competition game free from strife and turmoil and, in the other, for the ensuring of a future society in which generosity and unselfishness will produce authentic, responsible freedom.

3. Both capitalism and socialism agree that economic development must be scientific and rational. Both agree that there must be economic planning in which the principles of scientific and rational planning must be utilized to program future economic developments. The capitalist will want to limit the planning to the individual corporate structure; the socialist will want to extend it to the whole society; but both would agree that the technically trained, rational, scientific planner must make decisions about the future. "Scientific" and "rational" have very specialized meanings in this context, however. "Scientific" means the maximization of technical efficiency—producing the highest output for the least cost. The capitalist justifies such an approach in terms of his obligation to the shareholders, the socialist in terms of his obligation to the people, but both are interested in production. "Rational" means that one considers the individual members of the corporate body as essentially collections of productive skills. The capitalist entrepreneur is completely uninterested (at least in principle) in the life of his worker off the assembly line or even in his conversations and friendships on the assembly line so long as these do not impede his productivity. The socialist— particularly the totalitarian socialist—claims a much broader

interest in the activities, thoughts, and feelings of his workers; but nonetheless, it is work and work skill that earn a person a place in the socialist society. Indeed, in Red China one must validate oneself even if one is a college professor by putting in a certain amount of time in rural communes.

The rational and scientific approach to economic development for both capitalism and socialism, then, means the maximization of productivity in a work system in which the individual's primary contribution is taken to be his productive skills. There may be all sorts of enlightened personnel policies or management counsels with labor representatives, but, in fact, the productive enterprise is organized either on an assembly-line basis or with little concern for other aspects of the personality of the worker besides his productive skills.

Thus, farmers in China, in the Soviet Union, and more recently, Tanzania (which although headed by Catholic convert Julius Nyerere does utilize the communal farm approach) could be uprooted from their peasant villages and forced into collective farms in the name of economic rationality, whereas on the capitalist side of the fence the assumption of a more or less completely mobile labor market is taken for granted. Does your meat-packing plant close in Chicago? Well, you can always move to Omaha. Does your firm decide to transfer you from Rochester to Rotterdam? You'll probably find a comparable upper-middle-class suburb in either city. The more sensitive of the socialists will lament for the suffering of the recently collectivized peasants; the more sensitive capitalist will be sorry about the family disruption caused by the move from Rochester to Rotterdam; but both will shrug their shoulders. There simply isn't any other way.

4. Both the capitalist and the socialist will agree that what they both might call "feudal" social styles and patterns are evolving out of existence or collapsing in the face of the advance of "science." The greats of the sociological tradition— Tönnies, Weber, Durkheim—all noted, not without melancholy, the collapse of the archaic order. However, this collapse would be considered by the contemporary capitalist or socialist (or liberal humanist, for that matter) as not merely descriptive but normative, not merely the way things are, but the

way they should be. The particular should give way to the universal, ascription should give way to achievement, the sacred should give way to the secular, the diffuse should give way to the specific, the informal should give way to the formal, the heterogeneous should give way to the homogenous.

All the archaic, outmoded, and perhaps superstitious ties of localism, tradition, loyalty, rootedness, "irrational" differentiation (meaning differentiation based on anything other than economic class) simply do not belong in a modern, scientific, enlightened world. Transient man is the explicit goal of contemporary society in the view of the capitalist and socialist alike. For the capitalist, mature man operates on universal principles and is tied to society only by his obligations to the shareholders. For the socialist, mature man ought to be bound only by the commitments the state requires of him until, when human nature is remade, he may freely choose for himself. But the capitalist and socialist together reject as obsolete and superstitious the ties of membership and loyalty that bind one at birth. The family may persist, but the clan, the extended family, the neighborhood, the locality, the village, the church, all have no place in the modern world.

5. Both capitalism and socialism are future-oriented. The socialist is perfectly willing to impose sacrifices in the present so that prosperity and freedom can be enjoyed in the future, if not by the one who now must suffer, then at least by his successors and descendants. Similarly, the immigrant laborer in the United States would work long hours for low pay as long as he had the promise that the money he saved up and the education financed by his taxes would make a better life possible for his children. As Peter Berger points out in his book *Pyramids of Sacrifice*, both China and Brazil have mortgaged the lives of their people in this generation for the future. In China, political freedom is sacrificed so that the future may be free; and in Brazil, economic poverty is imposed on large groups of society that in the years ahead the whole country might be prosperous. The sensitive capitalist and the sensitive socialist may lament this suffering, but, again, how else is one to build for the future except to impose suffering in the present?

6. On the subject of the lesser-developed countries, there is also a fundamental agreement between capitalism and socialism. Neither sees any way in which poverty, ignorance, and hunger can be overcome unless the archaic social structure and the superstitious culture of the indigenous people are eliminated. Revolution must destroy the old structure and culture, must wipe the slate clean so a new, modern, rational, scientific social order can emerge. In the capitalist view, revolution is accomplished gradually and normally without violence by the technician of the multinational corporation, whereas in the socialist view revolution is usually both more abrupt and more violent, and is carried out by a technician who may be more guerrilla leader than businessman. But both the Moscow-trained terrorist and the Harvard-MIT-trained corporation executive firmly believe that they know far better than do the untrained citizens of the target country what is necessary to eliminate misery, the injustice, the hunger, and the poverty that afflict the country.*

7. Finally, both capitalism and socialism believe in large size and centralization. The socialist assumes the Politburo and the Planning Authority are responsible for the politics and the economics of the whole country. The capitalist makes no such theoretical assertions, but still seems driven by the logic of his system to build ever larger corporate combinations such as conglomerates and multinationals to maximize efficiency and to minimize "destructive" competition. And all competition, it turns out, is destructive—particularly, if it is price competition. It seems to be built into the logic of the scientific and rational approach to production that organizations should get

---

* Peter Berger wisely comments that the pertinent question is not capitalism or socialism but which kind of capitalism and which kind of socialism in what country. It is also frequently the case that the ideologies of capitalism or socialism are merely a rationalization for the exercise of political power by the ruling class that happens to hold that power. The ideology, therefore, is much less important than the power. Certainly some African, Asian, and more recently, South American countries that purport to be "socialist" are nothing more than military dictatorships with a few socialist trappings. For the average citizen of Brazil or Peru it doesn't make much difference if the military dictatorship in one is described as "right wing" and the other is described as "left wing."[5]

bigger and bigger and bigger. Whether you are a socialist or capitalist the argument for "economy of scale" seems to be unanswerable. It often turns out, of course, that an increase in size does not make for an increase in efficiency, but such results normally lead neither capitalist nor socialist to question the need for both expansion and centralization.*

Obviously, I have greatly oversimplified. There are many differences between capitalism and socialism both in theory and in practice. Peter Berger in his *Pyramids of Sacrifice* has done a masterful job of outlining these differences, but Berger sees the two systems converging in their agreement that the present generation must be called on to sacrifice for the good of future generations. In the previous paragraphs I have tried briefly to elaborate this insight of Berger's and to root it in a prior view that capitalism and socialism owe to their common eighteenth-century English Calvinist and Hobbesian ancestors of the nature of human nature, human society, and of human social and economic progress.

The most critical Catholic dissent has to do with the nature of human nature. Unlike the socialist, the Catholic is profoundly skeptical about remaking basic traits of the human personality. In the Catholic view of things, one does not cease to be wary or afraid of other human beings; one rather loves them despite one's fears. But while Catholicism is skeptical and reserved on the subject of remaking human nature, it takes a much brighter view of humankind in its present condition than does Protestantism. Humankind is deprived, perhaps, but not depraved. There is more that is admirable in man, as Camus said, than is contemptible. The flesh wars against the spirit, and the outcome is generally a toss-up, but Catholicism is inclined to bet on the spirit. Humankind is not fundamentally destructive, selfish, individualistic. There is a selfish, aggressive, destructive aspect to our nature; but there is also a

---

*Schumacher notes that in the early years of the Ford Motor Company, when it was made up of a hundred twenty-five people, a decision could have been made to shift from gasoline to steam power in the space of a few hours. Today it takes months to change even a single screw on the assembly line.

generous, trusting, and cooperative aspect to it, and Catholicism is more aware of and has far more confidence in that aspect of the human personality than does Protestantism. Though under no illusion about the present condition of human nature, Catholicism still sees a sufficient amount of goodness and generosity to call people to virtue rather than to compel them to virtue.*

The Catholic social theory, then, makes the fundamental assumption that you create social order by an appeal to humankind's cooperative disposition and not by force or by Hobbesian constraints. You sometimes have to back up pacific appeals by force, but society is not created by violence or maintained by force or even by formal social contract. It exists by definition when you have more than one social animal in the same physical environment.

Since it has a relatively more benign view of human nature, Catholicism can also take a more benign view of society. Social constraints, which in the Catholic view exist to reinforce and support the cooperative tendencies of social beings, are not so oppressive that one must keep them to an absolute minimum (as in the capitalist view of things) or that one need impose them to a maximum amount in order that they may eventually wither away (the socialist view). Catholicism is under no illusion about oppressive states and oppressive societies; it has fought some and, lamentably, has allied itself with others; but it would deny that society or the state are necessarily or fundamentally oppressive. Society exists not so much to restrain human selfishness as to facilitate human growth (though in the process it must restrain some selfishness). And the state is not the arm of oppression to remake human nature or to keep the competitive system going; it is simply society's arm for ensuring an atmosphere of peace and tranquillity in which flawed but basically good human beings can create and share common enterprises and activities by which they may stumble through life a little more easily. Such a view of state and society is

---

* At least in theory. In practice, of course, many Catholic leaders over the last two millennia have attempted to compel virtue. In so doing, however, they have been completely false to their own theory. As Thomas Aquinas tells us, virtue is acquired by frequent repetition of *free* acts.

relatively modest. The state is neither the necessary evil of capitalism nor the temporary evil of socialism, but a mixture of good and evil, like everything human; and under the proper circumstances, it is often more good than evil.

There is about this Catholic view of society and of the state something that may seem just a bit cynical. It is clearly utterly lacking in idealism, but it is also relatively free from disillusionment. The Catholic social theory expects more of both humankind and human society than does the capitalist and substantially less than the socialist. It never expects to see a paradise on earth, but neither does it feel the need to remain content with life in the jungle. It has been around for a long, long time; it modestly expects to be around for a long, long time to come.

The Catholic stands in utter horror of scientific or rational economic progress. He does not believe in Adam Smith's rational economic man. You never encounter people like that in the villages, the parishes, the neighborhoods, or, the Catholic social theorist suspects, anywhere in the world. Neither does he believe in economic man's first cousin, the *homo faber* of the large corporate bureaucracy. You conceptualize a human being, the Catholic social theory argues, as a set of economic needs or productive skills only if you fundamentally misunderstand what human nature is all about. Furthermore, if you organize human enterprise in such a way that your theory and your structure assumes that you have combined a group of productive skills for the maximum efficiency of output, you are not only likely to do terrible things to the human persons involved, you are also likely to defeat your own goals in the long run. You may try to ignore or to eliminate or even to destroy the nonrational and nonscientific residues that cling to your corporate bureaucrat and industrial worker. You can take him out of his village and put him on a collective farm, you can move him from Rotterdam to Rochester and back, you may even get him to parrot an abstract universalistic ideology of the left or the right; but in the real world you and he will still be caught in the web of intimate, informal, particularistic, diffuse relationships rooted in biology, propinquity, or shared beliefs. The sensitive capitalist and socialist will say that of course he understands that the human being is a total person and not just a collection of economic needs or productive skills, but the rational or scientific organization requires only economic needs and/or productive skills. One does not deny the other aspects of his personality, and one may be peripherally interested in doing what one can to see that his other needs are satisfied, but when push comes to shove, there is no particular reason to think that they are important either in satisfying the demands of the profit-hungry stockholders or the goals the planning board set up for the five-year plan.

The Catholic social theory obviously dissents. Human life is both an organic and differentiated unity. Human beings live in dense networks of overlapping commitments, relationships, loyalties, involvements. There is a pluralism of relationships in human society that constitutes, in Maritain's words, "organic heterogeneity in the very structure of civil society."[6] To ignore that organic heterogeneity even for the purpose of drawing up an organizational chart is not only to do violence to the people whose jobs appear there but also to risk the ultimate collapse of one's effort, because abstractions are not to be found on the assembly line or in offices of the bureaucracy. One cannot abstract human beings caught in relationships, committed in loyalties, and absorbed in beliefs, viewpoints, and prejudices. To forget that is to misunderstand everything.

The Catholic social theory, then, has a profound respect, one might say reverence, for the informal, the particular, the local, the familial. It does not believe that this delicate and intricate web of primordial ties that bind human beings together in dense and close relationships should be ignored or eliminated. It does not believe that evolutionary progress is moving the human race from particularism to universalism. It does not believe this for two reasons: first of all, its definition of human nature as social and relational does not permit it to see intimacies as temporary or transient or easily replaceable. Second, in all its dealing with the ordinary people who constitute its congregations, Catholicism encounters very few who are suitable for life in any "temporary" society. With rare exceptions, those transient citizens who can decamp from Rochester to Rotterdam to Riaydh, or from Cambridge to

Hyde Park to Berkeley at a moment's notice are unhappy and frustrated. Catholicism doubts that they are the leading edge of evolutionary progress—and it is skeptical that many human beings would want to live that way unless they were forced to.

The American Church in particular (if it ever bothers to reflect on itself) would be astonished at the way the life in the peasant villages of Ireland, Italy, and Eastern Europe were reconstructed in the slums of New York, Chicago, and Boston —perhaps they were not so much reconstructed as simply transplanted.

The Catholic social ethic does not believe that you should try to destroy the web of personal intimacy that every human being spins around himself. More than that, it also believes that you cannot destroy it. Abolish *Gemeinschaft* if you will, but it will reassert itself in the giant factory or the mammoth collective farm. Before you know it, it will be in control again, and its influence will be all the harder to deal with because your ideology forces you to deny its existence.

This argument is perhaps the most telling point that the Catholic social theory can make against both socialism and capitalism, for it is both an ethical and an empirical point. You should not try to destroy *Gemeinschaft*, says the Catholic society theory, and, besides, you cannot. It is a judgment that admits of empirical falsification or verification, and as we shall see shortly, the evidence is overwhelmingly against those who think you can dispense with or ignore the primordial, the particularistic, the local, the intimately interpersonal.

The Catholic social theory categorically rejects the notion that one can or should sacrifice the present for the future. It is outraged that anyone should suggest that you should. The end does not justify the means, however noble the end. A future material paradise of peace, prosperity, plenty, and freedom does not justify slave-labor communes, hunger, misery, torture, repression. The Catholic social theory takes this position in part because of its view of the nature and destiny of the human person created in God's image and called by Him to grow in knowledge and love. A creature who hungers for the absolute in the roots of his personality is not to be a pawn in a planner's program for economic development. For the Catholic social theory also knows that this benign future paradise cannot be counted on to appear. The New Class, like the old class, converts means into ends and becomes much more interested in preserving its own power and privilege and prerogative than in producing the New Order to which it is allegedly committed. With the observation of its own clergy and hierarchy succumbing to the temptations of power, Catholic social theory is under no illusion that other powerful bureaucrats, no matter how pure their original motivation, can ultimately escape the same temptations unless there are strong and effective legal and structural limitations on their power. The Catholic social theory knows enough about grand inquisitors to be suspicious of them. You do not build a better future by exploiting the present. The "pyramid of sacrifice" strategy really only provides a rationale for staying in power; it is both immoral and self-deceptive.

Because of its beliefs about human nature, about the organic and heterogeneous pluralism of human society, about the critical importance of the web of primordial relationships in which each person is enmeshed, and because of its convictions about fundamental dignity and the value of each individual person, the Catholic social theory must be profoundly skeptical of all attempts at "modernization" or "development" that purport to improve the material lot of people by destroying its culture and its social structure. Doubtless some cultures and structures are more open to growth and development than others. Doubtless, too, there must be changes in some societies if poverty and hunger are to be eliminated; but the Catholic social ethic has too much respect for the tenacity of tradition, the power of custom, the resistance of inertia, and the strength of fundamental belief and values to think that a collective farm, a multinational corporation, a giant steel mill, or a fleet of tractors can enjoy anything but short-range success when imposed on a people who view these innovations as fundamentally alien to their way of life. If you can integrate innovation into the culture and structure of a community, then the innovation may prosper, but if you tell them to jettison their values and forget their customs and embrace the new technology for increased food production, for example, they may elect for customs and values in preference to food (much to the astonishment of the Peace Corps volunteer, the socialist bureaucrat or the industrial technician, no doubt). You may dispense medical services in the Himalayas, New Delhi, and the southwest side of Chicago, and in each place you may use the most modern and advanced techniques of preventive and curative medicine; but you must never forget that you are delivering your services to an individual who is not an isolate, bereft of values and convictions. You are delivering them to a person who has value and worth in his own right and who is caught up in an intricate web of human relationships, commitments, and loyalties. Any attempts at social change, the Catholic theorist must argue, that disregard these facts about human nature are both morally and intellectually wrong—and they won't work.

Finally—and this may be the easiest way to tell the Catholic social theorist from the socialist and the capitalist—he is profoundly suspicious about size. Just as the capitalist in principle and the socialist in practice thinks larger is better, so the Catholic theorist can only respond that small is beautiful. Of course, one must avoid the romantic temptation to assume that small is invariably beautiful or better. A hundred people cannot support an airline, a country of small farmers cannot produce enough food to feed the world—or even one large industrialized society. "Too big" is not an absolute matter but a relative one, and from the perspective of the Catholic social theory something becomes too big when it is bigger than it has to be to do the job. The principle of subsidiary function is perhaps the central theme of Catholic social theory. It vigorously argues that nothing should be done by a larger organization that could be done as well by a smaller one; and nothing should be done by a higher bureaucratic level that can be done just as well by a lower level.

Perhaps the mistake of much Catholic social theory in the past was to argue as though the principle of subsidiarity was a philosophical deduction rather than an empirical observation. You keep things as small as you possibly can because they work better that way, there is more flexibility, better communication, more room for innovation, adaptation, and quick response to new problems. You decentralize decision-making as much as you can because those who are responsible for carrying out decisions participate in the decision-making process and because their motivations to see successful implementation will be much stronger. These are not merely ethical principles; they are empirically documented facts. Such facts are ignored today in the organization and administration of corporate bureaucracy, which merely proves that the blinders of ideology and habit can filter out critically important information. In the short run, giantism is efficient. You can maximize production quickly with "economies of scale." The only trouble is that the corporate organization is made up of more than just machines; it is also composed of human beings, and in the long run, economies of scale easily lead to diseconomies of human effectiveness. This fact has been proven time and time again, but it still does not seem to have sunk into the thinking of the theorists of either corporate capitalism or corporate socialism.

Catholic social theory would also argue (here with an approving nod to the Volvo experiments) that no matter how large the organization, it is immoral, erroneous, and foolish to treat it as though it were made up of atomized, isolated individuals. Even if you bring a group of complete strangers together to operate your plant, those strangers will set up informal social networks during the course of the first morning. Soon *they* will run the factory, not you. Also, you may drive the peasant out of his old village and set him up in a clean, new, efficient agricultural commune, and you may even threaten him with death if he doesn't live up to your standards of productivity, but that does not mean friendship networks will not emerge to deftly and subtly sabotage the goals set for you by the Central Planning Board in Peking, Havana, or Moscow. From the perspective of Catholic social theory, it is not a question of an organization without *Gemeinschaft* but rather an organization that recognizes and works with it.

The Catholic social theory differs from capitalism and socialism, for example, in its view of individual and class conflict. Capitalism and socialism assume that in the natural state of things individuals and classes are in conflict. In the capitalist society the state is the organ of the ruling class (though capitalists would be reluctant to admit that quite so explicitly); in a socialist society the state allegedly becomes the instrument of the oppressed class against the ruling class (though in fact it usually becomes simply a tool of the New Class). Both theories are uneasy about conflict within their own societies. Social and political unrest, or even too much diversity, is viewed by the capitalist as a threat to the stability of his society and the maintenance of high levels of productivity. The socialist, once he has gained power, considers political opposition to be counterrevolutionary and vigorously represses dissent. Both socialist and capitalist applaud conflict and competition in theory and do their best to repress it in practice —perhaps because both are impressed by the inherently unstable nature of human social institutions.

The Catholic theory, on the other hand, is much more relaxed about the stability of human institutions because it views them as based on the dense and intimate interpersonal networks of "lesser groups," which it takes to be the raw material of society. Since these lesser groups (family, local community, friendship circle, local church, neighborhood, etc.) are normally more cooperative than competitive, the Catholic social theory assumes a matrix of much greater social cooperation than do its two individualist social theory adversaries. Of course, even within much smaller groups there is competition (between husband and wife, parents and children, poker players and bridge players), though the competition rarely destroys the cooperative structures. Catholic social theory assumes that such competition is normally more healthy than not and is not greatly disturbed by it.

Precisely because it has much greater confidence in the positive and constructive forces that are at work—or at least can be at work—in society, the Catholic social theory is less worried about the society's capacity to deal with diversity, competition, and conflict in its "greater groups." It realizes that such competition can lead to instability and societal breakdown, but it does not necessarily do so. Hence Catholic social theory, unlike its socialist counterpart, sees no reason to repress dissent (however much it may have been repressed in certain Catholic states). Unlike capitalism, Catholic social theory is not worried that conflict between labor and management, for example, will destroy the industrial enterprise. After all, the Catholic theorist notes, labor and management do have common interests as well as diverging ones.

But if it takes conflict and competition for granted (even viewing them as good), Catholic social theory is deeply suspicious of those who deliberately set out to stir up conflict between classes—especially when this conflict seeks to make the opposing class the scapegoat, the enemy to be destroyed, the evil cause of all one's trouble. Thus the Catholic theorist must reject in principle the current epidemic of romantic scapegoating of certain "oppressor" groups—men, whites, older people, the Northern Hemisphere. For all his respect for societal networks, the Catholic theorist is absolutely committed to the worth and dignity of the individual person and cannot tolerate the arbitrary assignment of guilt or nonvalue to anyone because of a characteristic acquired at birth. Furthermore, such scapegoating ignores the mutuality of interests that such falsely opposed groups obviously have. Finally, the Catholic theory observes that in the lesser groups the normal state of relationships is a mixture of cooperation and competition, with the former predominating for the most part. To pretend that such relationships are not the raw material of all society seems to the Catholic social theorist to be foolish posturing.

At the grass-roots level then is competition between men and women, between young and old, among various ethnic groups. It has ever been thus, and the Catholic theory accepts that it always will be. Yet, for the most part, the individuals involved relate to one another with tolerance, affection, and even love. You can compete with people, the Catholic social theory observes, and still love them. In fact, love and conflict are correlates as well as contradictions. Those mass-movement leaders who think you can have effective conflict and competition only when you stir up hatred against an opponent (or class) that must be destroyed are quite literally, in the view of the Catholic theorist, doing the work of the devil. Furthermore, in the long run their strategy won't work, for it is not natural for women to view men as enemies *all the time*, or for the young to view their parents as enemies *all the time*, or even for one group to view another as enemies *all the time*. But the propagandists of class conflict demand total enmity against the oppressor.

The three ideologies differ in how they imagine the triangular relationship between self, state, and society. The capitalist self is private but also essentially economic and subject to the laws of the economic marketplace, which unfortunately may on occasion (or frequently in underdeveloped countries) impose heavy burdens on the self. The state is distinct from society and exists principally to see that the rules of economic competition are honored and fairly imposed within the society. The state may occasionally intervene to protect the individual self on the premise that it is necessary for the utilitarian purpose of promoting the health of the society. It is a bad thing for some individuals to be so overwhelmed by the power of other individuals that they cannot effectively compete. The utilitarian intervention of the state on the side of individuals is justified by the necessity of keeping competition among the various enlightened private self-interests fair and open. The state may also intervene, indeed massively, in order to help those corporate bodies whose welfare is essential for the good of society (such as Lockheed). Such intervention is justified on utilitarian grounds again, that is, the efficient operation of the marketplace requires that certain competitors be kept in the marketplace even when their own incompetence would lead to their elimination from the game without protection. Obviously such a conclusion is a long way from the laissez-faire of Adam Smith, but it is justified as being for the good of the marketplace. The state, then, is a policeman hired by the marketplace to enforce the rules and to guarantee its good by subsidizing and protecting certain competitors so they can remain within it.

The socialist view is almost exactly the opposite. It believes that, effectively, there is no difference between society and the state. The state speaks "for the people" and is identified with the people—or at least with that segment of the people sufficiently free from false consciousness to know the true needs of the people. Since the state is merely society organized or the advance guard of society, it follows logically that there is no aspect of society that is independent of state responsibility and supervision. The whole of human life, the socialist argues, is political and hence it must all be politicized. The state may yield to the self certain areas of privacy, but only because those private areas are not presently essential for achieving the goals of society, and particularly its economic goals, or because the state is too busy with other and more pressing demands to worry about certain private areas. In principle, however, everything is liable to state control—the arts, music, literature, radio, television, newspapers, religion, family life—all in the name of the ultimate good of the people.

In the capitalist scheme the state works for the economy; in the socialist scheme the economy and everything else in the society work for the state.

Both capitalism and socialism share the conviction that man in society must be conceptualized as a collection of economic and productive skills: in capitalism, skills used for his own enlightened self-interest; in socialism, skills used for the good of the people. The Catholic social theory disagrees systematically. The self is private, inviolable, sacred; its dignity comes from its ultimate nature and destiny quite independent of politics and economics. Society exists to facilitate the growth of the human person, and it may not violate the dignity and the integrity of the person, no matter how noble its goals. There are certain things the society may legitimately require of a person for the common good, but those requirements can never go beyond the line that marks off the private personal dignity of the self.

Similarly, Catholic social theory believes that the state is a tool of society by which certain aspects of the general welfare are promoted and facilitated. The state exists as an agent of the whole society, of the lesser groups within the society, and of the individual persons who make up both the lesser groups and the society. The state urges, exhorts, coordinates, facilitates, reinforces; it does not dominate. However, it does far more than just enforce the rules of the political game. It not only regulates competition, it also sustains, supports, and facilitates cooperation. A state operating within the Catholic ideology might intervene less than do the massive welfare states of the North Atlantic world, but it would intervene, I suspect, in ways that they do not to promote reconciliation and cooperation. It would play the "honest broker" role in a much more formal and self-conscious way than do most of the welfare states. The facilitation of collective bargaining, for example, by various government mediation and conciliation services in the United States would be an example of the kind of activity one would expect much more of in a state more strongly influenced by Catholic political and social ideology.

The word "anarchist" is still capable of striking terror into the hearts of many middle-class Americans. It calls to mind images of bomb-throwing radicals, political assassins, crowds rioting in the streets, barricades going up, black flags flying over churches, priests and nuns being massacred and mutilated, and social order collapsing on all sides. Occasionally, perhaps, we also have the image of the brave Asturian coal miner attacking a fascist tank with a Molotov cocktail during the Spanish Civil War. We middle-class Americans may not like communists, but at least the Marxist stands for law and order even though it is *his* law and *his* order. But the anarchist believes only in chaos, it seems to us.

Yet anarchism has a respectable intellectual tradition, including such adherents as Godwin, Proudhon, Bakunin, and Kropotkin. Only a tiny minority of the anarchists were men of violence. Anarchism steadfastly resisted Marxist socialism, to which it always and inevitably lost, primarily because its theory prevented it from imposing the organizational discipline that Marxist socialism demanded of its followers. The anarchist tradition, though it has in practice fought the Catholic Church many times, has much in common with the Catholic view of society. Both Catholicism and anarchism, for example, believe in the social nature of human nature and reject in principle the centralizing tendencies of the modern world. They differ, of course, on their view of the reformability of human nature. A Catholic is not as pessimistic as the capitalist about the nature of human nature or even as pessimistic as the socialist about the present state of human nature, but he cannot accept the easy optimism (or so it seems to him) of the anarchist about the ease with which spontaneous cooperation will occur when the shackles of oppression are tossed aside. Human nature may not be depraved, according to the Catholic, but it still must be treated with caution. Sinfulness does not make us totally evil, but it does leave us with strong propensities to evil, propensities the anarchist does not seem to understand. Indeed, the Catholic might remark that it is precisely the failure of the anarchist to understand the strong predisposition to evil in the human personality that has led him to make self-destructive mistakes in his conflict with the Marxist socialist. This failure has also led to the collapse of his communitarian experiments even in places like Andalusia, where the only really large-scale anarchist social experiment had some success before it was wiped out by Franco's invading army.

Writing in 1962, George Woodcock[7] conceded that anarchism as a political movement was finished, defeated by its own internal mistakes, by the inevitable centralizing tendency of the modern industrial world, and by the relentless opposition of the Marxists and then the Bolsheviks, as well as those socialists who had chosen to throw in their lot with the rigid, not to say ruthless, authoritarianism. But Woodcock argues that though anarchism has failed as a political movement, it still has validity as an idea, as a concept of "pure liberty" against which we can "judge our condition and see our aims," as an ideal to resist the centralizing state and to enlarge personal freedom and individual choice and judgment. The anarchist ideal, then, according to Woodcock, however impractical in the everyday world, still stands as a beacon for the "insistence that freedom and moral self-realization are interdependent, and one cannot live without the other. . . ."[8]

But since the appearance of Woodcock's book, a neoanarchist movement has arisen—chaotic, undefined, and unorganized (as anarchism almost necessarily must be). Social critics such as Ivan Illich and Theodore Roszak, some segments of the ecological environmental counterculture, disciples of Norman O. Brown, and the young and not-so-young people who have flocked to rural, desert, and occasional urban communes since the middle 1960s all more or less self-consciously have at least rediscovered the anarchist vision, if they have not rediscovered the anarchist theorists or bothered to read them. As long as the centralized state continues to encroach on the areas of personal freedom that are left in the modern world, an instinct toward anarchist rebellion will remain strong. Anarchist social theory, then, must be taken seriously not only because it has more supporters now than it did when Woodcock wrote his study and not only because it is a logical quadrant in our two-by-two table but also because it will be a recurring response as long as the centralized bureaucratic corporate state—capitalist or socialist—dominates the modern world. Indeed, one might reasonably hypothesize that the most powerful wave of anarchism in the future will not be exemplified by the German student revolutionaries who raided American post exchanges in the 1960s, for example, but the tribal undergrounds that will resist the right- and left-wing military dictatorships that dominate most of the countries of the Third World. The wise Third World autocrat may not mind if his people read Marx and Engels, and he will not be too disturbed if they read Maritain; but he should live in mortal terror of their dipping into books by Godwin, Proudhon, and Kropotkin.

The anarchist believes that human personality contains within itself all the attributes necessary for living in peaceful social concord. Human nature is naturally social, indeed social even before it became human. Because of its social nature, no man-made laws or positive institutions, and certainly no social contract, are required to create society. In fact, these positive institutions are the real enemies of society. Hence the anarchist opposition to Marxist socialism with its proletarian dictatorship and rigidly constructed utopian vision. The anarchist argues that human nature is perfectable, but he does not mean that it can be made perfect according to a neatly planned and executed program. Godwin contended that perfectability did not mean that human nature could be made perfect but merely that it was capable of indefinite improvement, a notion that, he said, "not only does not imply the capacity for being brought to perfection but stands in express opposition to it." In the good anarchist society, then, there is to be no compulsion at all.

So the anarchist is devoted to the cult of the natural, the spontaneous, the individual; and while he does not seek to reconstruct the past, nonetheless he can find in the past (very much unlike his Marxist opponent) examples that come close to the society he would like to create.* The anarchist vision, according to Woodcock,

> is a kind of amalgam of all those societies which have lived—or are supposed to have lived—by co-operation rather than by organized government. Its components come from all the world and from all history. The peasant communism of the Russian *mir*, the village organization of the Kabyles in the Atlas Mountains, the free cities of the European Middle Ages, the communities of the Essenes and the early Christians and the Doukhobors, the sharing of goods implied in the customs of certain primitive tribes: all these attract the anarchist theoretician as examples of what can be done without the apparatus of the state, and they draw him nostalgically to a contemplation of man as he may have been in these fragments of a libertarian past.[9]

The anarchist was a man of the nineteenth century and argued, of course, that his view is "scientific" and "evolutionary." But he is in dramatic disagreement with the Marxist in his view of peasant society. The Marxist would dismiss the primitive peasant society as "a stage in evolution already past; for him, tribesmen, peasants, small craftsmen, all belong with the bourgeoisie and the aristocracy on the scrap heap of history."[11] Yet the anarchist finds in the poor peasant proletarians the rough models, as well as the raw material for his future society; and it is precisely among the poorest of the peasants and other classes excluded from the general mechanization and

---

* In its attitude toward social development anarchism often seems to "float like Mohammed's coffin, suspended between the lodestones of an idealized future and an idealized past."[10]

modernization of the centralized industrial state that the anarchist attracts his strongest supporters—the shiftless and rebellious sections of the lower classes whom Shaw called the "undeserving poor" and Marx dismissed as the *Lumpenproletariat.* Anarchist leaders were of the country gentry, former clergymen and seminarians, and craftsmen and artisans—those whom Marxist revolutionaries in Russia (and Cambodia) liquidated. It is these people who fit nowhere into the neat pattern of Marxist social stratification: "As a result the anarchist movement has always had its links with that shadowy world where rebellion merges into criminality, the world of Balzac's Vautrin and his originals in real life."[12]

But while the anarchist may look to other societies for examples for what human nature can do, in fact he is not rebelling in favor of the past as much as he is "in favor of an ideal of individual freedom which belongs outside the present."[13] The anarchist dreams of a society that comes into existence as a result of the spontaneous will of all the members. Under such circumstances, social and economic affairs are administered by small, local functional groups. After an existing society has been decentralized, debureaucratized, and simplified, individuals will spontaneously federate themselves into communes and associations, and these in turn will spontaneously federate into regional units and overriding authorities. "In this organic network of balancing interests, based on the natural urge of mutual aid, the artificial patterns of coercion will become unnecessary."[14]

The anarchist is vigorously antidemocratic, for democracy insists on the sovereignty of the people and anarchism insists on the sovereignty of the person. Parliamentary institutions are wrong because in them the individual has abdicated sovereignty to an elected representative. Furthermore, the majority has no right to inflict its will on the minority. "Right lies not in numbers, but in reason; justice is found not in the counting of heads but in the freedom of men's hearts."[15] Woodcock cites Oscar Wilde as bespeaking the anarchist position when he said, "There is no necessity to separate the monarchy from the mob; all authority is equally bad."

* * *

The principal differences, then, between the Catholic social theorists and the anarchists is that the Catholic is much more cautious about human nature and much less likely to be convinced that all restrictive or coercive human.authority is necessarily bad. Furthermore, the Catholic may not like much of what he sees of the world, but he cannot accept the anarchist vision of destruction (peaceful or violent, depending on what kind of anarchist you are) as a prelude to a new beginning.

For while the anarchist would admit in principle that the only growth that matters is organic growth, he argues that the political, industrial and scientific world in which we find ourselves is so corrupt that one must begin almost from the beginning to construct a new social order. The Catholic theorist is skeptical about any "fresh new starts," believing that one begins not from the beginning but from where one is; hence he finds it very difficult to conceptualize the utopian visions or to utilize utopian rhetoric.

Still he runs the risk of being dismissed as utopian by those who rigidly hold to the left-right paradigm. There are, after all, only two ways to solve modern human problems: the state control of socialism or the independent marketplace of capitalism. A third way is merely a compromise somewhere between the two, and it is impractical if not impossible to derive a third way that is not a middle ground but is rather the result of introducing another vector. The Catholic social theorist is told that he is trying to turn the clock back by re-creating a feudal society with its organic and dense networks of human relationships. Impossible, the modernist contends. These dense networks either no longer exist or are no longer relevant to the organization of modern industrialized society. Therefore we must choose between the tyranny of the corporation and the tyranny of the state or hew out some middle ground between.

Three of the four ideologies in our two-by-two table would claim to favor individualists—capitalism, anarchism, and Catholicism. The socialist position is that a rigid communitarianism in the present is necessary for freedom of individuals in the classless, communist society of the future. But the other three positions are unwilling to sacrifice the individuals of the present for those of the future. The capitalist insists on the economic freedom of the individual at least, even if often such legal and economic freedoms are not very meaningful for the masses at certain stages of development of the capitalist system. The anarchist rejects all authority, other than that which emerges from spontaneous cooperation, as oppressive to the freedom of the individual. Hence the attempts to find an achievement of the Marxist ideal in Mao's China or Castro's Cuba indicate a total misunderstanding of that ideal by present-day "anarchists." Anarchism may be communal, but it is surely not communitarian.

Catholic individualism dissents from capitalist individualism in that it rejects the capitalist vision of the individual as isolated, egoistic, and pursuing his own enlightened self-interest. In such a ruthlessly competitive social jungle, the Catholic theorist would argue, one has freedom and vast wealth for a few individuals and misery and slavery for many others. It categorically rejects the immolation of individuals in the holocaust of a pyramid of sacrifice of the present in order that individuals of the future may enjoy a socialist utopia. It comes closer to anarchism in believing that human nature is communal but not communitarian and that the individual achieves most effective personal development as part of a dense network of cooperation, support, and affection—though it dissents from the anarchist by arguing that sometimes, given the propensities of human nature to evil, some individuals must be restrained from taking advantage of others. It also believes that political authority can facilitate, reinforce, and promote the functioning of the subsidiary social and political networks. It concedes that oftentimes civil authority does not do this, but argues that it can and should.

Thus the Catholic social theory would argue that there is no contradiction between individual and society, between person and community. It would contend that the propensity of many modern observers to see such conflict is merely the result of their looking at human society from a very narrow, rigid, and insensitive perspective. For the Catholic theory the goal of society is ultimately the enrichment and fulfillment of the individual person. The person does not exist for society, society exists for the person; but the person enriches and develops himself only through cooperative social interaction. The community and the larger society are not, in the Catholic theory, necessarily obstacles to personal development and freedom (as they often become in the anarchist theory) but the absolutely necessary conditions for and the matrix of such development and fulfillment. You cannot become fully human by yourself, Catholic theory would argue. Of course, both the community and the society often become obstacles to the development of full humanity; they must be reformed. Such is the nature of human nature and its propensity toward evil that community and society need reform, but it does not follow that they are necessarily evil; it follows only that they are part of the flawed, frail, but still improvable human condition.

In principle the Catholic social theory can coexist with a wide variety of governmental forms. However, a number of Catholic theorists in the 1930s and 1940s, particularly Yves Simon and Jacques Maritain, argued that there was a special affinity between Catholic social theory and liberal democracy (of the North Atlantic variety). For the Catholic insistence on pluralism, decentralization, personal freedom, and limitations on the power of the state seemed to have a special affinity with notions of civil liberties, pluralistic governments, and the limited authority of the state that emerged out of the Anglo-Saxon political tradition. Unfortunately very few American Catholics have bothered to reflect on the interpenetration of Catholic social theory and American political practice, which has been at the core of the American Catholic experience. The wards, the precincts, the neighborhoods of the urban immigrant world were the places where this interpenetration occurred; and with the exception of John Courtney Murray and, more recently, John Coleman, very few American Catholics have any respect for this fascinating event.

It is very difficult to see how something like the Catholic vision of the good communal society can happen in a state where there is no freedom of expression, no right of dissent, and no possibility of political opposition.

Thus the principal problem of dialogue that faces the Catholic theorist is to prove that the dense organic networks of society, which the modernization model argues no longer exist or at least are no longer important, still do exist and still are important.

Fortunately, the overwhelming burden of the social science evidence shows that they do and are.

CHAPTER 6

❦ ❦ ❦

Social Science
Data

THERE are two important resources that contemporary social science makes available to those protagonists of the Catholic ethic who are interested in resources. First of all, it establishes beyond doubt that *Gemeinschaft* is alive and well. Catholic social theory has argued resolutely for more than two hundred years that the primordial ties of family, friendship, and local community should not and cannot be destroyed. Both capitalism and socialism have assumed that evolutionary progress and scientific advancement either eliminate such ties or make them irrelevant. The evolution from the primary to the secondary, from community to association, from loyalty to contract, from folk to urban, and from sacred to secular was taken to be inevitable.

Beginning with Elton Mayo's Hawthorne studies in the late 1920s,[1] a massive amount of evidence has been assembled to indicate that the primary, the primordial, and the informal not only survive but keep the large corporate bureaucracies running, to the extent that these monsters run at all. It was the friendship group on the Hawthorne assembly line, for example, that determined the productivity standard. It is the small combat squad, held together by loyalty to the father-figure noncom officer that keeps the modern army going. Marketing decisions, the use of innovative drugs by doctors and innovative agricultural methods by farmers, and voting decisions all take place not in interaction between an isolated individual and the mass media but in small informal friendship groups into which various opinion leaders become the key persons in diffusing innovation.

The majority of American families still live within a mile of at least one grandparent, and siblings and cousins are still the people with whom visits are most frequently exchanged for a substantial part of the population. Urban research from the time of Robert Ezra Park to Gerald Suttles has emphasized the "urban village" (to use Herbert Gans's words) dimension of the ethnic neighborhood. More recent research shows the persistence of the neighborhood phenomenon even after one has crossed suburban lines. Informal but powerful cliques come into being in almost all large corporate bureaucracies, and if one wants to know what a decision that has come down the formal chain of command means, one plugs into one's favorite informal communication network to know how to react.

Only a pop sociologist such as Alvin Toffler or an abstract social theorist who completely ignores empirical evidence takes the myth of the massified society seriously. The alienated, anomic isolate may be found on the university campus or in the upper reaches of some of the large corporations, but Philip Slater's transient man and temporary society[2] are *rarae aves* indeed (and more recently Slater himself has turned away in abhorrence from the thought of transient man). I am unaware of a single responsible sociologist who has looked at the empirical evidence and still believes that. The world is not on a pilgrimage from the particularist to the universalist; it is rather a combination of both. There may be rather more universalist norms and relationships available now than there were in the past, but that simply is because there are more relationships. The particularistic has survived and indeed probably provides the warmth and affection and support that make universalistic behavior possible. Similarly, the existence of a much larger number of formal, stylized, specific relationships (the textbook case being that between the bus driver and the passenger) does not mean that these relationships have increased at the expense of the informal, casual, diffuse relationships of the past. Rather, what has happened is that simply the number of human relationships has increased. If anything, there may even be more primary group relationships than there were in the past. One is part of more intimate friendship circles (some of them perhaps even transcontinental or intercontinental) than were one's ancestors. Weep not for *Gemeinschaft*. It is alive and well and living in Midtown, Chevy Chase, Cambridge, and even Berkeley.

But despite the fact that virtually every social scientist to whom one speaks today will acknowledge the survival of primary-group relationships in the midst of the large corporate bureaucracies, the theory of the modern organization (capitalist or socialist) has not yet been fundamentally reconsidered and restructured to take this insight into account, almost fifty years after Elton Mayo's experiments. The so-called "human relations" approach to management is an option only after a corporation has managed its primary obligation to its shareholders. Profit-sharing, management-sharing, even informal work groups such as the Volvo experiments have been around for decades, but so powerful is the tenacious hold of the evolutionary model and the formal organization chart that no one really believes that the way we run universities, federal agencies, automobile companies, or public educational systems is insane.

But it is not merely the large corporate organizations that have remained fundamentally unperturbed by the social-science evidence about the survival of dense organic networks described in the propositions of my modernization model (Table II). Social science itself has been unable to absorb such evidence in its own theoretical structures. In the late 1950s and the early 1960s a number of major sociological schools contributed to what has been called "the rediscovery of the primary group." Parsons, Freed Bales, and their colleagues at Harvard, the late Paul Lazarsfeld and his students and colleagues at Columbia (in their studies of political and marketing decisions), and Edward Shils and his students and associates at the University of Chicago, all independently arrived at what was basically the same conclusion: primary-group relationships are essential in the maintenance of all formal bureaucratic organizations. Subsequently the demographic historians found the nuclear family at the *terminus a quo* of the modernization model, and the sociologists found the primary group at the *terminus ad quem*. Neither was supposed to be there according to the theory.

Another source of doubt on the evolutionary theory of modernization has been the research done by historically oriented sociologists (some of them, curiously enough, Marxists) on the actual modernization process that is going on in the "new nations" of the world that have emerged since 1945. Joseph Elder's "Brahmins in an Industrial Setting" and Manning Nash's *Machine Age Maya* uncovered little evidence of conflict between the traditional and the modern that is necessitated by the process of industrialization. Richard Lambert discovered that traditional values of security and primary-group loyalties were a strong element in the successful operation of Indian factories in Poona. Lloyd and Suzanne Rudolph, in their book *The Modernity of Tradition*, systematically and categorically question the applicability of the modernism model to political development in India. As Nash observes of Cantel (the Guatamalan town he studied):

> [It] is not the same society it was before the introduction of the factory, but it is still a going concern and still a distinct way of life, rich in local meanings and in patterns of social relations far removed from the kinds of societies which have invented and spread machine technology. Cantel's experience with the mechanisms of adjustment to a new economic form and its resultant pressures means at least this: factories may be introduced into peasant societies without the drastic chain of social, cultural, and psychological consequences implied in the concept of "revolution." The idea that social change involving new forms of production is necessarily wasteful in human terms finds no support in Cantel.[3]

In a powerful and important paragraph Nash concludes not only that tradition is not an obstacle to industrialization but that industrialization will not be effective unless it respects tradition:

> To judge from Cantel, a people's ability to accommodate to new cultural forms is intimately related to their actual and felt control over their social circumstances. The sense of control seems to stem from their freedom to choose how they will combine the new elements, and to discard or accept the innovations as their consequences become clear. Cantelese did not begin to absorb the factory into their communal life until force and the threats of force were withdrawn. They began to come to the factory as workers when they realized it as a means of implementing some of their goals.[4]

The Rudolphs are even blunter:

> The assumption that modernity and tradition are radically contradictory rests on a misdiagnosis of traditional societies, a misunderstanding of modernity as it is found in modern societies, and a misapprehension of the relationship between them.[5]

The Rudolphs analyze the persistence of caste in the modern Indian political structure, the persistence of traditional charisma in the impact of Mahatma Gandhi, and the persistence of traditional Indian law in a "dual system" of law. They observe that all three are examples of how the traditional and the modern mix and blend, with the modern building on the traditional rather than replacing it.

Clifford Geertz, in his classic analysis of the religion of Java,[6] demonstrated that in Indonesia even modern party politics, allegedly based on universalistic ideologies, actually became closely identified in practice with ethnic and religious group loyalties at the village level. You could not mobilize Indonesians for modern politics unless you appealed simultaneously to traditional values.

The strongest argument that industrialization leads to "modernization" has been made in a six-nation study by Alex Inkeles and David H. Smith.[7] The two authors found that in Argentina, Chile, East Pakistan (now Bangladesh), India, Israel, and Nigeria there was a broad pattern of behavior connected with factory experience that could properly be called "modernization." However, they excluded from their definition such components of the classic modernization theory as weakening of family ties, decline of religious activity, and lessening of concern for the aged on the grounds that such variables might increase with industrialization—which in fact they did—leading to "modern" religion, "modern" family, and "modern" care for an aged relative. The Inkeles-Smith project, a monumental and ingenious enterprise, thus does establish that something happens, and it is important. Included in that "something" is more active citizenship, greater economic aspirations, heightened sense of personal efficacy, greater assumption of personal responsibility, greater valuation of education. But these things do not occur as a result of the decline of certain basic and traditional allegiances.

The research of political scientists such as the Rudolphs and anthropologists such as Geertz on the Third World countries provides an excellent model for the reexamination of what happened in western Europe during its industrialization era. If we can leave aside a model of "modern man" that assumes that he is different in some fundamental way from his ancestors and design our research on the basis of a model that assumes only that contemporary man is not much different from his ancestors but has acquired some new skills, perspectives, and experiences, as well as a much longer life expectancy and greater social and geographical mobility, we may understand the meaning of the Industrial Revolution in the West much more clearly than we do when we use the evolutionary modernization model.

Thus demographic historians in their rediscovery of the nuclear family and private property at the beginning of modernization, the sociologists of the primary group in their rediscovery of the persistence of *Gemeinschaft* in the modern world, and the political scientists who analyze the "developing" nations find not modernity replacing tradition but a marvelous combination of modernity and tradition intertwined with each other. All three strike a shattering blow at the theory of modernization.

Yet the demographic historians keep parroting the term "modernization," even though their data do not support the modernization hypothesis, and sociologists continue to speak of modernization even though they themselves have discovered the primary group at the *terminus ad quem*. "You want to turn the clock back," they say to the Catholic ideologue who talks about the dense organic network of human social relationships. The response (perhaps *ad hominem*) might well be, "But you just told me that the clock has not gone ahead."

"But something has changed," says the sociologist, pointing to the modernization model. Certainly something has changed. But one of the most important changes runs in exactly the opposite direction to the modernization model. It is precisely because of the complex differentiated, highly organized structure of *Gesellschaft* society that contemporary human beings have available to them a much greater number of intimate, personal, diffuse, informal, intense relationships than was available in an earlier era. Far from reducing the dense organic network of intimacy, modernization has made it even denser. My great grandfather living in Ireland may have had *Gemeinschaft* relationships with his parents, his spouse, his children, his cousins down the road, a couple of other friends in the parish, and maybe (but by no means certainly) his parish priest. His descendants in Chicago have a much wider variety of intense personal relationships, most of them limited by geography, but some extending around the world.* "But," says the sociological modernizer (or the nonsociologist for whom Alvin Toffler has become Scripture), "these relationships are not nearly as deep as the old ones back in County Mayo."

It all depends on what one means by "deep," of course. If one

---

* Those of us who get caught up in the world-travel circuit know how it is possible to have close friends whom one sees only once or twice a year and with whom it is nonetheless able to resume relationships just where they were left off. There are some interesting aspects of these transcontinental and transoceanic friendships. Simply because people see each other so rarely they tend to invest substantially more emotional energy—and sheer time—during those interludes when they are in physical proximity to one another. Furthermore, since one is not sharing life space on a day-to-day basis in such relationships, one can take risks that one would be hesitant to take when dealing with one's next-door neighbor.

speaks in the physical or quasiphysical sense, it is surely true that the old intimacies of the premodern world had immense power. One simply did not leave them, no matter what. Divorce did not occur, and to leave the close village life in Europe for another country, to say nothing of another continent, was for all practical purposes, to die. (Indeed, "American wakes" were held in Ireland for natives who were migrating to the United States.) As far as their family and friends were concerned, they were dead. One can now sunder such relationships fairly easily; one can end a marriage or move with much greater ease. One knows now that a new set of relationships can be created, and the telephone and the jet airplane enable one to sustain the old relationships at least in some fashion. Moving is not easy and neither is divorce, but both are possible. Relationships do not have the compelling physical depth they used to have. Furthermore, because intimacies can be sundered today more easily than they could in the past, there is a dimension of unease in even the closest relationships which was not present in the past—though then higher death rates made life itself more uncertain.

And yet one could make the case that the psychological depth of some relationships is much greater than in the premodern world. We have learned how to be much more open and vulnerable to our interaction partners; we become more deeply involved humanly and personally in nonfamilial relationships than many of our ancestors did even in their familial ones. A marriage today, even if it should end in divorce, probably involves more vulnerability and intimacy than many premodern marriages that did not end in divorce. I am not suggesting that there is more love today than in the past—that is both an unprovable and absurd suggestion. I make the much more modest claim that there seems to be much more self-conscious, interpersonal vulnerability and hence much greater opportunity for psychological depth if not physical depth in contemporary relationships than there were in premodern ones. The modernization model must once more be stood on its head. Not only are there quantitatively more *Gemeinschaft* relationships for modern man than there were for his predecessors, they can also be qualitatively deeper and richer. The real problem of modern man is not that he is the isolated, alienated individual lost in the lonely crowd of the mass society, the real problem is that there are likely to be far greater demands for intimacy and vulnerability placed upon him—and far richer rewards promised—than he has developed the personal skills to respond to. One has to be intimate, one has to relate openly and honestly, one has to experience spectacular orgasms whenever one makes love. What has become possible, easily becomes obligatory. Furthermore, society, which has created the kind of affluence and leisure that in turn has made possible such demands for intimacy, has unfortunately been unable to restructure itself either to socialize young people in the skills necessary to respond to such demands or to organize the productive, distributive, and consumption sectors in such a way that they do not notably impede response to the demands of a neo-*Gemeinschaft* culture.

The other resource that social science makes available to Catholic theory is evidence that Catholics do in fact behave toward human society in a way that suggests the Catholic social theory is not merely a theory but a pattern of behavior more likely to be absorbed by Catholics in their early childhood socialization process than by others. The encyclicals, Hilaire Belloc, Maritain, Mounier, are explicating in a formal and reflective fashion certain convictions about human nature and society that most Catholics unselfconsciously and unreflectingly carry around as templates for interpreting experience and shaping behavior.

In careful sociometric studies, Professor Edward Laumann of the University of Chicago has discovered that, with all other pertinent variables taken into account, Catholic friendship patterns curved like a closed circle while Protestant friendship patterns more resembled spokes on a wheel without the wheel.[*8] If Laumann's careful work can be sustained in other communities besides the one he studied, one might be able to argue with considerable confidence that there is a

* A somewhat oversimplified picture:

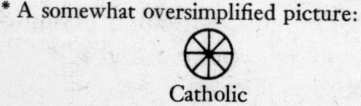

Catholic

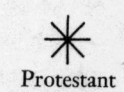

Protestant

proclivity in Catholics toward forming communal groups that seems not so strong in Protestants (or at least some kinds of Protestants).

Professor James Q. Wilson of the government department at Harvard University, in his classic study of Irish police sergeants, has the following extraordinary quote about the behavior of Irish sergeants:

> Of course; no question about it. I have often thought, half-seriously, if you want to change a police department rapidly and effectively by putting new men at the top who will be loyal to the commissioner and do everything by the book and according to standard operating procedures, you could just about throw away the elaborate personnel tests and screening procedures we have devised and simply promote the northern European officers—the Germans, Scandinavians, English, and the like. You would get the same desired result with less time and money. [Q: Why is that?] It's hard to explain. It's not that they are necessarily any more honest than the Irish Catholic officers or that they are any smarter. It's more that they have a much greater and more obvious commitment to some set of rules, standards, or general principles as a way of doing and seeing things. The most striking fact about the Irish Catholic command officers in this department is the extent to which they rely on personal loyalties and the exchange of personal favors as a way of doing things. If there is a perfectly legal, routine way of doing something, you can almost be certain that many of your Irish Catholic officers will prefer to do it through some informal means instead. They deliberately step outside the formal system to do things informally. There is often, in fact usually, nothing at all wrong with what they are doing, it is just that they seem to feel more comfortable working through 'contacts,' intermediaries, and friends."[9]

Wilson suggests, quite properly it seems to me, that the reason for this behavior might be attitudes acquired by the Irish during the Penal Times, when the indirect, the informal, the casual—answering a question with another question—were the only ways to escape British tyranny. (It is also true, however, that the Irish language is an extraordinarily gentle one, avoiding abrupt, dissonant words and phrases; there is no word for hello or good-bye, for example.)* Finally, it may also be the case that whatever the past explanations are, the Irish police sergeants have a much better feel for how to get things done than a rigidly structured formal bureaucracy. If you don't put anything on the record, and if you don't let anything go through official channels, and if you answer with a question or a wink of the eye or a nod of the head, you have a lot more flexibility. Your subordinate or superior is free to do what he wants and still, if worse comes to worse, and somebody tries to impose the rules or the book, then you can shrug your shoulders and say, "Who me?" Maybe some of those sergeants could be made vice presidents for administration of corporations suffering from bound muscles and hardened arteries.

Professor Terry N. Clark attempts to explain the strong relationship between the proportion of the Catholics in a city, especially the proportion of the Irish, and public expenditures.[10] The Irish, he says, are particularists. Particularism is a tendency to treat "persons in terms of personal characteristics and continuing social contacts." Universalism, by contrast, is a "tendency to adapt general rules (of law or medicine or whatever) to interpersonal situations; abstract principles are applied to specific 'cases' or 'clients' by the ideal universalistic judge or bureaucrat. For example, a person unhappy with street cleaning could (universalistically) call the department of public works. Or (particularistically) he could call his friend the precinct captain—with perhaps identical results.[11] Clark quite properly points out that noninstitutionalized behavior is the behavior of anarchy and chaos (quasi-Hobbesian); but in fact, according to Clark, situations in which there are no formal rules and formal organizations are frequently regulated by exchange behavior, "specific relations and exchanges of favors among particular individuals. . . ." He adds, "values and norms are at least vaguely present in almost all social situations. But so are personal contacts. The Irish ethic implies a tendency, when there is a choice, to lean more toward the personal contacts for guidance than toward the values and norms."[12] Professor

---

* Substitutes are "peace to this house" or "Jesus and Mary be with this house."

Clark does not suggest that the Irish are the only Catholic groups to have such particularistic style of operation; he does not address himself to other Catholic groups. And I would not suggest that the Irish have a monopoly on implicit and unself-conscious Catholic social theory; they merely happen to illustrate it.

The political participation research of my colleagues Sidney Verba and Norman Nie provides another strand of evidence.[13] These two political scientists devised four different kinds of political participation: campaign activity, voting, civic behavior, and communal behavior. Civic behavior was characterized by belonging to and being active in various community organizations; communal behavior was characterized by direct personal contact with political leaders or their intermediaries. One would expect that if the Catholic ideology is to be found in the ordinary Catholic population, Catholics would be high on communal activities and Protestants high on civic activities. The latter, in other words, would engage in establishing and maintaining new structured organizations to achieve their goals, while the Catholics would emphasize existing, informal communication links. The evidence fits just such a pattern. Protestants and Jews were high on civic behavior, and Irish, Polish, and Italian Catholics were high on communal behavior. There were some intriguing variations, however. Jews were high on campaign activity, and Protestants were high on voting. The highest voters of all, however, were Polish Catholics, and the highest of all on campaigning as well as civic and communal behavior were the Irish.

Finally, in analysis directly occasioned by the reflections contained in this paper of data collected by my colleagues Kathleen McCourt, David Greenstone and their team of researchers, I was able to test directly for the presence of some sort of "neighborhood ethic" among Catholics (see Table VI).[14] If indeed Catholics are disproportionately likely to have a conviction about the importance of a dense and organic network of informal personal relationships, one would expect the Catholics to be more deeply attached to their city, their neighborhood, to know more neighbors in the neighborhood, to share neighborhoods with members of their family, to have

TABLE VI.
Protestants, Catholics, and Neighborhoods

	Protestants (n = 308)	Catholics (n = 587)
Born in same city	53%	79%
Not planning to move	54%	68%
Move outside Standard Metropolitan Statistical Area	31% (of those who are moving)	23% (of those who are moving)
Like neighborhood	66%	74%
Know "many" neighbors	53%	62%
Some family in neighborhood	25%	38%
More than half of close friends in neighborhood	16%	25%
"Friendly people," most liked neighborhood attribute (spontaneously mentioned)	10%	15%

a higher proportion of their close friends in the neighborhood, and to spontaneously describe "friendly people" as what they most like about their neighborhoods. All of these suspicions (I won't glamorize them by calling them "hypotheses") were sustained by the evidence.

Catholics do have a stronger loyalty to their neighborhood, a loyalty that we would have predicted on a priori grounds from our knowledge of the style of religious reflection of the Catholic high-tradition theorists and the Catholic social and political ideology as it has been described in this volume. Of course anyone who has ever lived in a neighborhood would have taken such findings almost for granted.

The contribution of the social-science evidence, then, to our argument is this:

While there have been major changes in science, technology, transportation, communication, and the complexity of the social structure, these changes do not seem to have eliminated or even to have reduced the importance of intimate, personal, informal, nonrational, local, permanent, loyalty-based relationships. On the contrary, if anything, there are more such relationships and more interpersonal psychic investment in them. Furthermore, such relationships have immense influence on the corporate social structure and indeed may be essential to keep it running. Finally, the persistence of such relationships seems to be especially marked in that one religious group whose political and social ideology vigorously denies either the possibility or the desirability of minimizing such ties.

Something has happened all right. But "modernization," as the term is normally understood, turns out to be a very bad description of it.

The work of Laumann, Wilson, Clark, Verba, Nie, and the McCourt-Greenstone team does not "prove" beyond all doubt the existence of an unselfconscious Catholic view of human nature and society that is widespread in the Catholic population, but their work does at least raise the possibility that the high-tradition theorists are not so much deriving their social perspective from abstract principles as they are commenting on "instincts" about human social behavior that Catholics absorb very early in the socialization process. Nor need these instincts be formally theological in the sense that they are derived from clear and explicit doctrinal propositions. I would suggest as a working hypothesis that the low-level tradition of Catholic social theory takes its origin from primordial intuitions about the nature of human nature and the nature of human society that have been part of the Catholic tradition for centuries. The police sergeant, the politician, the union leader, the bishop in a multiethnic diocese, the pastor in a multiethnic parish are all equipped with a set of templates for organizing, interpreting, and responding to behavior which have been carried along in the Catholic tradition without much formal awareness for a long, long time.

It is the fashion in contemporary American Catholicism to be ashamed of most of these people. The bishop who balanced the various pressures of Americanization and ethnic consciousness in the early decades of this century, the parish priest who stood in the back of the church and walked the streets on cold winter days, the precinct captain who could tell you within one or two votes how well he'd be able to deliver his precinct, the machine politician, the cigar-smoking union leader—all of these seem somehow reprehensible in an age of universalistic principles, reform politics, and new politicians. But the turn-of-the-century bishops kept the Church from falling apart, and the union leaders, perhaps more than anyone else, are responsible for the de facto redistribution of income in America. The urban political machine at least sees that the snow is shoveled, the garbage picked up, and the streets repaired. Indeed, if one compares the achievements of the precinct captain, the machine boss, the parish priest, the brick-and-mortar bishop, and the union leader with the achievements of corporation presidents, socialist bureaucrats, university administrators, and such new-style politicians as John Lindsay, one begins to suspect that those unselfconscious practitioners of the Catholic social theory may not have been such complete failures after all.

Loyalty may be the nub of the whole matter, for loyalty is a particularistic, diffuse, informal, communal virtue. The theories of both socialism and capitalism are terribly reluctant to appeal to it. For capitalism the motivating force is enlightened self-interest, for socialism it is commitment to the goals of "the people"—meaning, of course, the people in general and not a particular band of brothers with whom you happen to be interacting. For the Catholic social theorist, however, loyalty is the critically important virtue. "If you can't be loyal to a friend," remarked one Chicago political lawyer, "you'll never be loyal to an ideal." One of my university colleagues remarked—quite appropriately I think—that in his world view, exactly the opposite was the case. Here we have the quintessential confrontation between the particularists and the universalists. Both the capitalist ethic and the socialist ethic believe it is "bad" for human beings to take their primary motivation from such old-fashioned, reactionary, tribal, and feudal ideals as loyalty. Passion for justice, for equality, for improving the lot of the people, or simply for making profit are admirable, progressive, scientific, rational motivations; but loyalty seems more in place in a jungle village or among the Plains Indian tribes or in the rock-strewn fields of western Ireland.

The Catholic social theory argues that the human person is a composite of soul and body, with body rooted in place and involved in a network of relationships that will always respond to the primal appeal of loyalty. Furthermore, the Catholic social theory will contend that any human institution that attempts to ignore the importance of loyalty or, even worse, tries to eradicate it as human motivation will find itself in trouble.

The capitalist and socialist theoreticians share the conviction that modern scientific, enlightened human beings can and should derive their principal guidelines and motivations for social behavior from ideas and ideals. The Catholic social theorist believes that contemporary humankind and every version of humankind we are ever likely to know will be far more easily and readily and effectively and permanently moved by people than by ideas (and "people" means, as noted before, something quite different from "the people").

I must insist once again that Catholics have no monopoly on this perspective. The new ethnic political theorist, John Schaar, for example, would insist on loyalty at least as strongly as any Chicago Irish politician. And communal ties are as important to E. F. Schumacher as they were to G. K. Chesterton. To call the social theory "Catholic" means that it is a theory that the Catholic tradition, among others, still carries, however implicitly and unselfconsciously. Even if there are now no practicing Catholic social theorists, and even if the social activists abandoned the theory for a combination of America-hating and soft-core socialism, the low tradition still survives out in the parishes, the precincts, and the trade-union locals. How long it will survive is another matter.

CHAPTER 7

Policy Implications

"**Y**OUR paper falls apart at the end," a number of readers of an earlier version of this essay have commented. "Your policy recommendations simply don't live up to what you have promised. They are too gradualist, too pragmatic, too much concerned with modifying the system rather than establishing a new one."

Or as James Coleman remarked in a National Opinion Research Center seminar, "How are you going to get really effective power for the new precinct captains with which you propose to honeycomb the large corporate bureaucracies?"

The answer to Coleman is that I don't know. And to the Catholic critics who expect me to be concerned with overthrowing a system and designing a new one, I answer that the pertinent question is not whether one comes up with a new system or even whether one makes policy recommendations that stir the passions of potential revolutionaries; the question of policy recommendations is rather whether they are the recommendations that flow from a Catholic social and political ideology.

I do not propose to attempt to construct a utopia or even a blueprint. Previous attempts to do so out of the Catholic social theory, the so-called Industry Council plan of the 1940s and 1950s, were not notably effective.* Moreover, I find myself completely incapable of utopian visions or rhetoric. I do not doubt the power of utopian models to stir up passionate commitment, but I find myself strongly doubting their power to accomplish much of anything; and I think it is far more important pragmatically and experimentally to start from where we are and push off in a general direction rather than to define long before we get there what things are going to look like in precise detail once we do arrive.†

Moreover, I do not think that by its very nature the Catholic social ideology is compatible with utopia-construction (with all due respect to Thomas More). In an organic analogue things grow naturally from where they are to where they are going to be. It is far more important to support and sustain the natural and organic growth processes than to try to constrain them to fit a preconceived model that is rigidly imposed upon them. A play-it-by-ear pragmatism may characterize Catholic politicians precisely because they are Catholic. Utopias are often found in the minds of intellectual visionaries, but it is the relationships of ordinary people, the Catholic social theory would suggest, that ultimately shape the structure of a society.

Finally, there has been precious little thought over the last twenty years about what society would look like if one ap-

---

*The Industry Council plan was a blueprint for control of large corporations by tripartite boards made up of unions, management, and the public (usually meaning government), not unlike some of the co-responsibility practiced in various ways in Germany, Sweden, and Yugoslavia today. It was one possible practical plan derived from Catholic social theory, but not the only possible one, and not one for which there was much support among American workers (nor does there seem much support today). In retrospect, the plan suffered from being "too concrete"—it equated a perspective and a point of view with a concrete practical program.

† And here I differ quite substantially from my friend Ivan Illich. Illich's critical perspective is, I suspect, rather similar to my own, but Illich, by choice, has become a utopian critic, leaving it to those who remain after he has headed for the local airport to figure out how the society he has just demolished is to be put back together again. It is one style, and a highly effective one rhetorically, though not so effective politically. However, it is not my style, and that is that.

proached it from the frame of reference of the Catholic social ideology. Catholics and non-Catholics alike have accepted the capitalism-socialism continuum and have absolved themselves from any need to speculate about social reforms that would seem desirable if one introduced another vector into one's model. Even the Christian democratic parties of western Europe, which have held political power intermittently in many countries since 1945, have not produced the kind of intellectual ferment that would have led to constructive and creative speculation about a fundamentally different approach to social reform from that offered by the moderate wing of social democrats (from whom the Christian democrats of the left are mostly indistinguishable). In other words, it is no time for utopias, surely, and no time even to expect an answer to James Coleman's realistic question as to how we provide the new precinct captains with clout.* It is time now for the more modest task of beginning to think about such issues and to raise questions. Therefore in this chapter I propose to do little more than to raise questions.

All the programmatic or policy implications in this section

---

* Coleman's question came after a long dialogue in which I was proposing that all large corporate bureaucracies should be staffed by "precinct captains" who can make sure that the bureaucracy does for its clients what it is supposed to do. Thus in your local Ford dealership there would be a hot-line telephone that you could pick up and scream into when you had been cheated on a repair bill or when they would not replace your lemon: "Make these s.o.b.s fix my car!" It would be relatively easy to set up such a protest network, but Coleman's pertinent question is, How do you equip the people who man the protest posts with the power to force the local dealer to be responsive? In the old days, precinct captains traded service for your vote; indeed, they were brokers, bearing the influence of your vote to other parts of the bureaucracy that needed it to stay in power. What do you have to offer the Ford Motor Company? Well, you can take your business to General Motors, except Ford is well aware that General Motors is providing equally unsatisfactory service, and that for every customer it loses because of its lemons, it will pick up one because of General Motors' lemons. So why worry?

I'm afraid I don't know the answer to Coleman's question. But the point is that because I don't know it, it does not follow that answers cannot be found—particularly if enough people begin to systematically and seriously think about alternative models for social organization out of the perspective of a Catholic social ideology described in this book.

are the result of the reflections of one observer viewing political and social events (largely in the American context) from the perspective of Catholic social theory. They are not deductions from the theory and are not to be equated with it. Other observers of good faith, good will, and professional skills might make different recommendations in the light of the same theory. Catholic social theory is not a set of principles from which one can derive with a priori logic practical policies and programs. It is rather a set of fundamental insights and assumptions about human nature and society that provide a perspective for looking at social reality. This distinction has not always been remembered in the past (or in the present either), and elaborate social schemes have been deduced from the theory without any reference to careful research on the problems for which the theory is supposed to be prescribing. Frequently it has also happened that such programs or policies are invested with a special and unique classification as *the* Catholic answer, thus putting the Church and its gospel solidly behind a contingent social program. The basic pluralistic bent of Catholic social theory must include a tolerance for a pluralism of answers to complex problems and a rejection of the pose of those who claim to have the *only* acceptable Christian or Catholic answer.

The most that can be expected of these concluding recommendations is that they may provide some stimulus for thought. I propose to raise these topics under seven headings. The points covered are neither systematic nor exhaustive. They do not represent either a coordinated or a comprehensive statement of what a society would look like if a Catholic social theory had some influence. My illustrations are those of one sociologist, influenced now by a self-conscious and explicit grasp of the Catholic social theory, would raise questions about structural changes in his own society.

1. *Delivery services.* Most of the goods and services that we use in modern urban America, be they a welfare check, police responses to a burglary, a new car, a dishwasher, or the education of our children, are delivered to us by the large corporate bureaucracy claiming to be organized and administered ac-

cording to the principle of rational, scientific theories of humankind and the society. The mail comes late, the dishwasher doesn't work, the car is a lemon, and the education the kids get is rotten; and if you don't like it, there's not much you can do about it because there aren't any alternatives available. And in truth, it doesn't much matter whether the society you are in is communist or capitalist. Corporate bureaucrats have the power and the services. If you want the services, you get them from them, or you don't get them at all. In Mao's China, there is periodically a chance to get even with bureaucrats by having things such as the great proletarian cultural revolution, only it turns out that after the revolution you have the same bureaucrats or new ones with the same mentality back in power. Bureaucrats are not evil human beings; they are in truth not much different from the rest of us. Or, to look at the matter from a different perspective, most of us are, in one of our manifestations, bureaucrats. We are caught in a bind where we are forced to administer laws or impose regulations or render service not to human beings but to "cases" or to "clients" or to deal with "shareholders" or "labor" or "management." Almost all corporate bureaucracies work so badly that it ought to give one pause about the fundamental theory on which the organization is based, but no matter how many people have given pause, the theory still dominates. Both the "case" and the "caseworker" (to use the most dehumanized possible labels to the interaction process) are caught in the same dehumanized and dehumanizing structural system. Can anything be done to change it?

First of all, is it possible to decentralize delivery of services in such a fashion that they accommodate to the local community and not vice versa? In its remote origins the "maximum feasible participation" clause of the war on poverty may have had something like that in mind. In practice, of course, it often meant that reformers outside the neighborhood and militant but nonrepresentative people from within the neighborhood used government money to promote discontent and "revolution" against the government, which was paying the bills, and the society, which was providing the taxes from which the government was paying the bills. Maximum feasible participation often simply meant "neighborhood-based protest." There may be something to be said for neighborhood-based protest, though if it is subsidized by the government one begins to wonder about its authenticity. But neighborhood-based, -administered and -controlled delivery services are something rather different. In backward cities such as Chicago, if your garbage isn't picked up properly, you can pick up a phone, make one phone call, and be reasonably confident that it will be picked up properly the next day. Unfortunately, you have no such control over what goes on in your children's school or what response General Motors will make to the latest model Chevrolet lemon that you've bought. Ralph Whitehead, speaking of the "communal social system," suggests, a little facetiously, that all large corporations should be organized the way the Cook County Democratic machine is organized, "minus the corruption." It's a startling thought, but the world might be a much better place if the school principal, the manager of the Chevrolet agency, and postmaster, yes, even the parish priest had to walk the streets of the neighborhood to make sure his constituency was happy, as the Chicago precinct captain (that last vestige of urban "bossism") must. My colleague William McCready, in his discussion of the "neighborhood ethic," quotes with obvious approval the Polish proverb on a precinct captain's desk: "GOYA-ARD," which is an acronym for "Get off your ass and ring doorbells." It would, I think, be a much better world if more of the people working for, let us say, the Social Security Administration, had to go around each day ringing doorbells to see if their "cases" were happy.*

Modern bureaucracies were designed in such a way that the "case" or the "client" would be completely at the mercy of the bureaucrat. "Rational" administration, as Max Weber pointed out long ago, means *sine ira et sine studio* ("without anger or favoritism"). In practice, though, such administration

---

* Since I first wrote this chapter there has been a considerable increase in discussion in both government agencies and private-foundation circles about local (neighborhood) delivery systems. Indeed the neighborhood is just now (fall 1976) very "trendy," almost "chic." It is too early to tell whether this is a major social change or merely a fad.

really takes place *sine cognitione et sine amore* ("without knowledge or love"). The client is completely at the mercy of the bureaucrat. The latter has something the former wants or needs or desperately requires. The former, on the other hand, has absolutely nothing to give back. The bureaucrat's knowledge, his professional motivation, and his commitment to the goals and the regulations of his organization are supposed to make this a human and humane interaction situation, but the result is frequently tyranny. (In the private sector, one can of course take one's business elsewhere—as if it mattered in our noncompetitive automobile industry whether you go to buy your car from Ford or General Motors. Both corporations assume that customer dissatisfaction cancels out and that it is uneconomic to spend much money or time or energy worrying about it.) Is it possible to restore in this relationship some of the principles of exchange theory to which Professor Terry Clark referred in the passage I cited earlier? Instead of abstract professionalism, could one have, in a case-caseworker interaction, an exchange of positions that would give the case some power over the caseworker instead of vice versa? Could, for example, the case have the right and obligation to fill out some evaluation of the caseworker's performance, an evaluation that would be taken seriously by his superior and that would go into a file to be examined when the caseworker is up for promotion. Thus, the case has the opportunity to return one favor with another. Such an idea may seem archaic, if not anarchical, to the theoreticians of both capitalism and socialism, to which I would reply that it seems to me a lot less traumatic than a great proletarian cultural revolution.

Might it also be possible to equip the individual who must deal with the corporate bureaucracy (any corporate bureaucracy) with a certain amount of clout. For those unfamiliar with the vocabulary of Chicago politics, "clout" is an exchange commodity. It is a certain amount of influence that one has to enable one to get things done, to see that one's needs are responded to sympathetically.* Unfortunately, most of us lack

---

* These needs may be something thoroughly dishonest, like a passing mark in a test in which one failed, or thoroughly honest, such as repairs to the street in front of your house to which you have every right. The

clout when it comes to dealing with the corporate giants. We don't have any contacts; we don't have any friends who have friends; there is no mysterious personage who our brother-in-law knows to get things done; there is no "mutual friend" to whom one can appeal beyond all bureaucratic authority.* Clout, in effect, is the right to appeal, but the right to appeal quickly and effectively to someone who can cut through red tape and reports in triplicate to get you what you need or want or have the right to in short order. You may call the man with clout an ombudsman or an expediter, if you want. I'm not about to insist that he be labeled precinct captain so long as everybody acknowledges that it is the function the precinct captain, at least ideally, is supposed to play. Let me illustrate the importance of clout with a specific incident. A certain neighborhood on the southwest side of Chicago is going through the process of racial integration. It is made up for the most part of single-family units of large, solid, and gracious construction. Its streets are curved, tree-lined, its lawns carefully landscaped, its people proud of their homes and community. Once the dormitory suburb of the Protestant management of the packing-house industry, then the domain of the upper crust of the Irish middle class, Beverly has more recently become one of the most cosmopolitan neighborhoods in Chicago, with people from many walks of life and many different backgrounds—whites, blacks, Asians, truck drivers, Federal judges, surgeons, blue-collar workers. Blacks are moving into the neighborhood, but so are white families. Property values are inching up despite the recession. From fear about their future, the residents of Beverly have shifted to confidence. The blacks and the whites of the neighborhood have been working together for peace, harmony, interracial friend-

---

outside view of Chicago politics is that most exercises of clout are corrupt and dishonest. However, most clout interchanges are in fact just the opposite. They are situations in which voter and political leader make sure the administrative bureaucracy works for the mutual advantage of both politician and the voter. Obviously, the system doesn't work perfectly and is subject to abuses, but then so is every other system.
* "Mutual friend" was a code phrase used in some Chicago telephone conversations to refer to a personage who was otherwise called sometimes "himself," or more frequently, simply "da mare."

ship. Local volunteer services are excellent, and the community has an increasingly active cultural life. The tide seems to have turned, and it would appear that Beverly could make it as a long-term stable integrated neighborhood.

One of its major assets was a suburban railroad line that put Beverly within a half-hour of the Loop. Suddenly, and without warning, the Illinois Commerce Commission ordered the line closed because some of the tracks were "unsafe." Since the railroad was in bankruptcy, there was no way the line was going to be made safe. And when was this death sentence issued? Two weeks before May 1, the day when apartment leases expired. The destruction of the last stable, integrated neighborhood on the southwest side? That didn't make any difference. Bureaucratic rules had to be obeyed.

In fact, there was no danger because the tracks in question are unsafe at fifteen miles an hour, but the trains go over the dangerous sections at ten. It makes the trip to the Loop a little slower, but not nearly as slow as riding a bus or fighting expressway traffic. The Illinois Commerce Commission didn't care; rules were rules; and why the rules didn't apply six months ago, or two years ago, but only two weeks before moving day? The ICC felt no obligation to answer the question.

Within twenty-four hours the mayor had made his feelings on the subject known, the Regional Transit Authority had met and appropriated funds for the repair of the track, and the ICC reluctantly backed off and gave the line a "two-week reprieve." The word went out, "That line will be closed over Milton's dead body" (referring to Milton Pikarsky, the chairman of the Regional Transit Authority). Clout had saved a neighborhood.

The illustration is fascinating because Daley had delayed for almost a year the effective operation of the RTA by insisting that if his man Pikarsky wasn't chairman, then there wasn't going to be any chairman and no operating RTA. He was roundly criticized by the liberal Chicago media and the Lake Shore aristocracy for "playing politics" with the RTA. The salvation of Beverly from the blundering dunderheads of the ICC made it clear why he was playing politics. No mayor of

Chicago can afford to have an institution as powerful as the RTA working in his city if he doesn't have some clout with the RTA board.

You don't have to use the word, but in practice, anyone who wants to deal effectively with the impersonal monsters of large corporate bureaucracies had better have clout.

2. *Review.* The rational and scientific approach, be it of corporate capitalism or corporate socialism, argued that planners, policy-makers, and administrators should be technically trained experts, the best men possible in their fields, completely immune from the necessity to engage in "electoral politics." The theory, of course, is that intelligence and technical skills are not merely useful assets in corporate bodies but the only things that really matter. Let us take three examples of what this means in contemporary America.

a. The Internal Revenue Service. Few people would disagree that the IRS is one of the most arrogant, vicious, and evil bureaucratic organizations the world has ever known. It has almost totally unrestrained power to oppress individuals and to repress those who dare to criticize them.* It uses spies, informers, sometimes even liquor and women. It maintains quotas of "productivity" for its investigators and auditors, and harasses thousands of individuals arbitrarily and vindictively each year. The result of the IRS's adversary approach to the taxpayer is that the standard advice a good accountant gives a taxpayer caught in the adversary role is to claim everything he can and then take his chances, advice that of course makes an already bad situation even worse. Does this mean that the IRS is presided over by vicious or evil men? On the contrary, the administrators and officials are probably some of the most honest, responsible, and competent people in the government. They are caught in a system that almost inevitably produces exactly what the IRS is, despite the good will of its personnel, a classic validation of Lord Acton's famous dictum.†

* Even writing a sentence like the last one, should I be brave enough to publish it, practically guarantees me an audit by the IRS.
† Some American supporters of socialism in other countries argue that while American bureaucrats may be insensitive and humanly incompetent,

b. Historians may well know the recession phase of the business cycle during 1976 as "the Arthur Burns recession." The brilliant, sophisticated chairman of the Federal Reserve Board was convinced that the real economic problem facing America was inflation and that it had almost singlehandedly created the pressures that have led to the downturn that occurred. Indeed, Burns' power as chairman of the aloof, non-political, professional Federal Reserve System was so great that in holding such a belief he could almost by himself cancel out the effect of a tax reduction voted by Congress in April 1975. The argument here is not that Burns was right or wrong (my own inclination is to think that he was probably more right than wrong); the point is that there is reason to question whether one man should ever have so much of restraining power in a society of free men and women.

c. Despite the United States Catholic Conference booklet on income and equality in the United States, most well-informed economists doubt that there is enough "flab" in the American tax system to provide revenue in the foreseeable future to finance many of the obvious new social requirements of our society. Revenues for these new programs, if they come at all, will have to come from the curtailment of other programs. However, it is hard to curtail any existing program because government cash outlay generates its own constituency, both within the bureaucratic structure and among those who benefit from the outlay. Rarely does anything ever get phased out even if there is no longer a need for it or if it is not working or if it is counterproductive. The right people in the right agencies see the right administrative assistants of the right subcommittee chairman, and the program goes on its merry way.

Ought it not to be possible to institute a system of review whereby periodically agencies like the IRS or administrators

---

and that American bureaucratic structure (such as the postal service) is disastrously inefficient, such is not the case with socialist bureaucrats in other countries because your typical Cuban or Vietnamese or Chinese (or whatever other ideal country it happens to be currently) bureaucrat is motivated by a passion for service of "the people." This is mostly baloney: a bureaucrat is a bureaucrat, and the IRS man hands out the same line about public service as would the Maoist mandarin in China.

such as Arthur Burns or programs such as community mental health or policies such as tax deduction for mortgage-interest payments* would be reviewed by the American public and either approved or disapproved? Ought it not be possible, for example, to extend the idea of the jury system to include review of government policy decisions and bureaucratic operations, say, every five years? The argument of both the capitalist and the socialist administrator would be that you can't trust the people to understand the complexity of the issues at stake. I reject that argument categorically. All the evidence we have from survey data about the sophistication of the American people leads me to believe that they can understand even quite complicated political issues. What a review panel or jury would need is to talk to their clientele in plain English, something that many of them would find painful, if not almost impossible.

How could such panels be formed? Could not one select a national sample of, let us say, a thousand Americans a year before the Federal Reserve System or the Internal Revenue Service were up for review? Could not this panel be paid by the government to spend a substantial amount of its time learning about the issues at stake in such a review? Could not such a panel then make recommendations to the Congress that would not necessarily be legally binding but that would still have tremendous moral power? Would not such a system provide extremely important feedback and control mechanisms for the bureaucracy and substantial political power for those congressmen who have to justify to their constituents some unpopular votes? This scheme may not be feasible technically (though it would take some persuading to make me believe that), but the vast and sprawling federal bureaucracy needs some kind of review by the whole nation—even if that means putting Arthur Burns up for reelection every five years. It may well be that the public will agree with Burns that inflation is a more serious problem than recession, and I am not suggesting that the public be polled on such things as margin requirements or discount rates, but I am saying that the public ought

* Which provides a far greater subsidy to housing than do any direct government housing programs.

to have the power to review those who are allegedly its servants but who frequently act like they are its masters.

3. *Personal dignity*. The Bill of Rights, which was written into our Constitution, was adequate for a society in which there were virtually no large corporate bureaucracies, but it desperately needs expansion to deal with a situation in which most of us are for most of our lives the victims of large organizations against which we have no defense. Should we not be guaranteed by our Constitution responsible and prompt service from all large corporate organizations, public and private? Should we not be guaranteed the right to appeal an arbitrary decision of a school principal, an Illinois Commerce Commission, a local Chevrolet dealer? Do we not have the right to clear, intelligible language, to rapid communication up through the bureaucratic hierarchy, and even to a system of public defenders, paid for by the bureaucracy, when we appeal against this harassment? Should there not emerge a whole new system of equity that would force the large organization we work for or deal with to treat us with respect and reverence and intelligence and understanding. Obviously, such a system of restraints, checks, and balances would drive the front-line agents of most corporate bureaucracies up the wall, for they are caught in a triangle made up of clients' demands, administrators' requirements for productivity, and rules designed to deal with cases or clients and not human beings. But the pressures such additions to the Bill of Rights could generate might force profound and systematic rethinking of the way we organize human behavior in a complex industrial world. If you are the isolated individual trying to deal with an arrogant, insensitive, powerful agency (private or public), it doesn't matter much whether the society of which you are a part proclaims itself as socialist or capitalist. It's bad news either way, and you can't fight city hall, particularly with a system that is designed to eliminate the corruption that might be involved if you had some friends in city hall.

4. *Freedom of choice*. One of the best things for the health and efficiency of any human organization is competition. Socialism eliminates competition by attributing it to greed. Cap-

italism eliminates competition by setting up monopoly. Socialism doesn't want a political opposition because that provides
the people with a choice. Capitalism is content with economic
opposition in frills and advertising, but shies away in horror
from competition over anything so crude as price. But, in fact,
if you want to protect freedom and dignity of the individual
person and the inviolability of the intimate and primordial
communities in which he is enmeshed, one of the best ways to
do it is to provide him with a choice. If an agency or organization is faced with going out of business unless it serves its
client effectively and efficiently, you'd be surprised how much
harder it works to keep its clients happy.*

No one likes competition. It makes you work harder, it
makes you eliminate the fat from your budget, it keeps you on
your toes, it forces you to be on the lookout for innovation. It
requires instant reform (*ecclesia semper reformanda* is a great
idea, though ecclesiastical bureaucrats are no more enthusiastic
about it than anyone else).

Hence, the introduction of freedom of choice to the world
of bureaucratic service is not exactly received with warmth by
any bureaucrat, and the governmental voucher system by
which the individual citizen or local community could choose
among different forms is greeted with an underwhelming response from government agencies. Public-school administrators would be opposed to the voucher system even if there
were a way that Catholic schools could be excluded from it. It
is not scientific or rational or efficient to give individuals or
communities freedom of choice. It makes things messy, irregu-
lar, inconsistent, and we like to have a neat, orderly society,
don't we?

5. *Family*. A capitalist theorist may argue that the family is
really none of his affair and that what someone does with his
wife and children is just none of the large corporation's busi-

---

* In this respect, the Cook County Democratic organization is not well
served by its Republican or Independent Voters of Illinois liberal
opponents who rarely give it opposition serious enough to worry about.
That the mayor always worried was a commentary on how completely he
believed the political truth that you never take anything for granted.

ness; on the contrary, for the corporation to invade the privacy of the home would be a horrendous offense against human freedom. The socialist may equivocate, depending on how authoritarian he is, but in practice socialist governments don't really see the family as their responsibility. What these approaches have in common is the assumption that the actions of the large corporate bureaucracy, capitalist or socialist, have no impact on family life. If you don't have a family policy, the argument runs, you are not affecting the family. In fact, the most profound impact the family has ever felt has come from the bureaucratizaton of human living that separates husband from wife and parents from children for most of the waking day—a situation that our ancestors would have found both incredible and intolerable. If one believes, as do not a few contemporary intellectuals, that the family is evolving out of existence, such evolution is a good thing and one need not be concerned about this development. Catholic social theory believes that for most human beings nothing is nearly so important as their family, in terms both of their conscious concern and of their unconscious impact on their behavior. Solid ethics and solid economics require that society be concerned about what its economic structure is doing to intimate relationships between parents and children, husband and wife. A number of questions must therefore be asked from the viewpoint of Catholic social theory (or at least of this Catholic social theorist).

a. Are there ways in which husband and wife, parents and children can spend more time together, particularly, if it be possible, together in productive work—at least more time together if they want to be together, for compulsory togetherness is as absurd as compulsory nontogetherness. How much of the work, particularly of today's professionals, could be done in the family house? Is the daily commute to and from the office really all that important? Could it not be limited to three days a week with relatively minor reordering of how society operates? Is the cottage-industry concept that obsolete? Are there not some kinds of production that could just as well take place in the family garage or backyard, or in a neighborhood vacant lot? Schumacher suggests that we might learn something from looking at the techniques of the cottage industries of a century ago.

Is it really necessary in the early stages of a career, in a relationship between the husband and wife, and parents and children, when they are at their most critical time, to keep the young professional away from his spouse (and more recently, her spouse) for extraordinarily long hours of work? Does anybody really accomplish anything in the professional world after he has worked a forty-hour week or even a thirty-two-hour week? Are not the absurd hours that professionals demand of themselves and especially of their junior colleagues an initiation ritual and an affectation rather than anything that is economically or organizationally necessary? Instead of requiring a seventy-two-hour week from a young professional, might it not be socially wiser to impose an absolute limit of thirty-two hours and ban the bulging brief case on the commuter train? Such a ruling would work havoc on the long expense-account lunches, but that might not be a bad thing for society either.

Can ways be found to permit husband and wife to work together in the same environment? That question sounds so absurd only because we have forgotten that most families the world has ever known have taken it for granted that husband and wife share work together. People increasingly marry those whom they meet in the work environment or in training schools preparing them for similar professional careers. It ought not to be too difficult to arrange things in such a way that husband and wife can share the same work milieu at least for part of the week—if they *want to*.*

Most of these suggestions seem bizarre, but only because we take for granted the assumption common to both capitalism and socialism that it doesn't much matter either for the good of the human person or for the whole society whether the family is scattered all around the metropolis through most of its waking day. Quite apart from its concern about the morality of sexual relationships and the transmission of religious

---

* Having endorsed the principle of a woman's equal right to a career in *Letters to Nancy* in 1961, I trust I will be dispensed at this point from repeating my oaths of loyalty to feminist goals.

values to children, the Catholic social theory must vigorously insist that any healthy society is deeply concerned about forcing husbands and wives, parents and children to part from one another. The good society will of course leave available the option that some family lives are much happier if they don't have to put up with one another through the whole day, but that's not the point. Now they don't have any choice either way. The old argument whether the family is the basic unit of society or not is largely irrelevant to this concern. However basic the family may or may not be, for most people it is still their most important intimate relationship. To make that relationship transient and temporary, a time of weariness and physical exhaustion on all the people involved is both crazy and evil.

It also probably seems absurd to suggest limitation on work, but most Americans work too long trying to make up with quantity for what they guiltily feel they lack in quality. It is very doubtful that the efficiency of society would be greatly impaired if the professional class was rigidly limited in the number of hours it works, and, indeed, the efficiency of society might be notably improved by longer vacations, more long weekends, and perhaps even a four-day weekend once a month. Compulsory sabbaticals might be a good idea too. All such nonworking times would make it much more likely that people would think, reflect, and give spontaneous creativity a chance to develop. Society can't make people think or reflect, much less make them be creative, but at least it can stop them from working or, perhaps more precisely, create a situation where if they work they have to do so in solemn secrecy. The Catholic social theory is convinced that you will have better human beings and more efficient workers if you have human beings who at least have a chance to think and reflect and create if they want to. Maybe Catholicism gave up its opposition to servile work on Sunday too quickly. The prohibition of servile work was once introduced to defend the ordinary serf against the demands of feudal lords who felt that, owning the serf body and soul as they did, they could demand from him unlimited work. The modern serfs are not so much the industrial laborers (not at least in the capitalist society) who are guaranteed time off but the professional class, which has no such guarantee—and might at first be afraid to make use of one if it were available. It is quite possible that the communal anthills in China would also profit from sabbath and feast days.*

The Catholic social theory firmly and constantly celebrates diversity. The society in which particularism is taken for granted is a society in which there is diversity automatically; and a social theory that believes that that which is special and unique and particular about each of us is worth preserving is necessarily committed to diversity. If you impose on society the fundamental Catholic principle of subsidiarity, you will automatically reinforce the creed of diversity because you will push decision-making down the ladder of corporate bureaucracy, for local and personal and particularistic factors will weigh more heavily. The word "pluralism" runs all through the literature of Catholic high social theory—papal encyclicals, Maritain, Mounier. It has to, because the emphasis on localism, subsidiarity, and informal and primordial ties necessarily produces a heterogeneous society. Catholic social theory will insist on the need for a higher unity that binds the various diverse groups together in a concern for the common good, and it will not deny the difficulties encountered sometimes in harmonizing the conflicting particularistic interest, but it believes it is much healthier for society to go through debate, dialogue, and even conflict necessary to generate a broad social consensus among diverse groups than for some higher authority to try to impose from above both consensus and a homogeneity on a society. The Catholic social ethic assumes that pluralism is good, that diversity is better than uniformity, and that unity is achieved through consensus and integration and not through homogenization. But it would argue that, even if such things were not positive goods, they would at least be necessary because you're not going to be able to homogenize human beings even if you thought it was a good

---

* And of course the sabbath as introduced in the Decalogue for the protection of workers, women, and slaves against the demands of the tribal chieftains. The new tribal chieftains are the technicians who dominate both the capitalist and the socialist society.

idea to try. Catholic social theory in the United States therefore must be committed to the understanding, protecting, and
celebrating of diversity while at the same time seeking for the
mechanisms of consensus and coalition that will integrate a
heterogeneous but variegated and fascinating republic.

It does not follow, of course, that Catholic social theory will
endorse all manifestations of diversity or all claims of those
who say they speak for ethnic groups or every manifestation
of pluralism. It will especially be suspicious of those advocates
of pluralism who are pluralistic "against," who look for scape-
goats or enemies to blame for their own problems or to validate their own uniqueness. He who attempts to turn groups in
the society against one another is, from the point of view of
Catholic social theory, no better than he who tries to achieve
unity by artificially imposing uniformity and homogeneity.
Both fail to recognize the organic unity of society, a unity that
comes from the integration of complementary parts. Society is
not an organism like the individual human body, but Catholic
social theory finds the model of an integrated but differentiated organism superior to the model of either a jungle or an
anthill.

6. *Localism.* Both because of its respect for primordial ties
that bind human beings together and because of its commitment to the principle of subsidiarity, Catholic social theory
vigorously defends localism and regionalism against the demands of metropolitanization—whether the metropolis be the
city or the national metropolitan center. Within the city, the
neighborhood is of absolutely decisive importance, and the
failure of most urban planners and most urban administrators
to pay attention to it at all is a reflection of the intellectual
bankruptcy of urban planning and administration. The welfare
department of New York City, for example, is concerned with
providing housing for the hundreds of thousands of people
living the strange, bizarre life of welfare dependency. If that
means dumping them in neighborhoods in the northwest
Bronx that are fighting for their lives, well, that's too bad. The
welfare department has a job to do, and it's tough on the
people who live in the northwest Bronx, who are probably

white ethnic racists anyhow. And if the courts are going to impose busing in the Boston area, well, of course you bus black children into South Boston, where the schools are bad to begin with and where the people have neither the sophistication nor the money to cope with such integration. They, too, are white ethnic racists and richly deserve what they get. Indeed, the whole court-ordered integration system that has dominated our approach to urban problems for the last decade doesn't give a damn about neighborhoods. A concern for a neighborhood school is written off as racist. A death sentence to a threatened neighborhood leads to a shrug of judicial shoulders. Build public-housing sites in the suburbs, subsidize suburban integration, oppose metropolitan integration so that the suburbs will have to take their due proportion of minority students? Don't be silly. It's in the suburbs where the federal judges and liberal lawyers live who are responsible for the integration suits in the first place.

The result, it would appear, is more segregation, as increasing numbers of people exercise their option to get out of the jurisdictions where schoolchildren and neighborhoods are considered to be pawns who can be moved around the map at the whim of a federal district judge (like the one in Detroit who thought that it was by no means unreasonable to expect kindergarten children to spend an hour and a half in the bus every day). Catholic social theory will not be opposed to court-ordered integration, but it will suggest that the worthy justices ought to at least show greater awareness of the full range of issues involved and take the responsibility for breaking down the artificial barriers of city limits that allow some people to escape the cost of racial integration. It might not be too much to ask the federal judge to consider that the order that he has issued may lead to more segregation rather than less; nor would it seem to be too much to ask that governmental policy-makers as well as intellectual and cultural leaders realize that, however desirable court orders and laws are, they are not enough to achieve social consensus and that they are indeed counterproductive to such consensus when they select out certain groups to pay the costs for discharging the guilt feelings of other groups of the society. Above all, Catholic social theory must insist that it is perfectly understandable that neighborhoods are important to people. One need not be a racist to defend one's neighborhood against threats from hostile outside forces. As Gerald Suttles has pointed out, the neighborhood is, by definition, a place to be defended.

It is extremely unlikely that judges, social planners, policymakers, urban administrators, or anybody else is going to take the neighborhood seriously—especially when Catholics, who owe more to the neighborhood than any other urban group, have yet to produce a single theorist who can write convincingly about the importance of a neighborhood as a decisive unit in metropolitan differentiation and integration, at least not since G. K. Chesterton wrote *The Napoleon of Notting Hill*.

On the contrary, most of those (outside of Geno Baroni's National Center for Urban Ethnic Affairs) who have anything at all to say about neighborhoods from the Catholic perspective are content with repeating the Cambridge–Hyde Park cliché about "white ethnic racism." It is fashionable among the Catholic elites to talk about "creating community," but those communities are reserved only for those who understand the rhetoric of the community creators—which is probably less than 1 percent of our Catholic population. Those preexisting communities, the neighborhoods, combined as they are of the precinct and the parish, are ignored, written off, and denounced. An authentic Catholic social theory must argue that the neighborhood is an absolutely indispensable unit in all urban planning. Either social policy assumes responsibility for reinforcing the strength of neighborhoods or it will largely be a waste of time. What will happen, of course, is a continuation of the kinds of decisions and policies that were typical of John Lindsay's administration in New York: neighborhoods are seen as obstacles to be bulldozed out of the way of the great schemes and the grand designs dreamed up in the skyscraper planning offices on Manhattan Island.*

A Catholic social theory will also insist, I think, on the importance of regions. Schumacher makes the interesting ob-

* For a brilliant account of one such plan, see Mario Cuomo's *Forest Hills Diary: The Crisis of Low-Income Housing*. New York: Random House, 1974.

servation that if Bismarck had annexed all of Denmark, Copenhagen would have become merely a provincial city within the German Reich and would have lost all the distinctiveness and unique charm it has as the capital. One may also make an interesting contrast between Dublin and Belfast, the latter little more than a north-of-England industrial town, the former beginning to recapture some of the cosmopolitan graces it had at the end of the eighteenth century, when it was the third largest city in Europe. Or it might be pointed out that a city with the size and resources of the city of Brooklyn would be far more important than it is if it were any place else in the world than across the East River from Manhattan. It is not merely that the intellectual and cultural life of the satellite cities in a country are destroyed when their talent is creamed off and attracted to the metropolis. An equally serious result of national metropolitanization is that the unique contribution that regional centers could make to the national life is destroyed or ignored. Catholic social theory must at least wonder if it is necessary for one city to be the cultural and intellectual center of the country. Must all publishing houses, all TV networks, all national journals be published between Greenwich Village and Central Park? Is it a good thing for the industries or for the country that the principal producers in the idea industry be that provincial in their dwelling place and viewpoint. Poking fun at the Midtown intelligentsia is like shooting ducks in a gallery: one can hardly miss, but beyond the fun-poking there is a very serious problem. Midtown is not the United States, but by default it speaks for and to the rest of the country and interprets the country to itself and to the rest of the world. Such a narrowness of base and perspective isn't good for anyone, and it is especially bad for the idea industry (and such places as Berkeley, Chevy Chase, and Cambridge are in many respects New York suburbs). Such metropolitanization of talent is built into the logic of both capitalist and socialist conviction that power must necessarily be concentrated not only in the hands of the elite but in one physical place.*

---

* All of this is, of course, hard on the real New Yorkers who don't live in Midtown and who, unlike a substantial part of the Midtown elite,

7. *Size.* Catholic social theory looks at American society with the preliminary assumption that almost everything is too big. It would insist on far more rigorous interpretation of the antitrust laws—and far quicker implementation of them. It would advocate an upper limit on the size of all educational institutions—in particular, universities—and demand that the present multiversities be broken up administratively into independent component colleges. (If it works at Oxford and Cambridge, why not at Berkeley or Champaign-Urbana?) It would shift the obligation of proof not on those who are against larger size but on those who are in favor of it. You would have to prove beyond any doubt at all that an increase in the size of an institution would make it both more efficient and more humane. Catholic social theory would insist that the assumption is against size until the contrary is proved.

It would want to see a significant segment of the national resources devoted to experiments with decentralization and the breaking up of the musclebound, tongue-tied, barely breathing corporate giants. Nothing should be done in a neighborhood parking lot that could be done just as well in the backyard; nothing in the small factory that could be done just as well in the parking lot; and nothing in the large factory that a small one could handle; nothing by a conglomerate that an independent firm could do just as well. All the dynamisms of capitalist and socialist bureaucracies alike go in the opposite direction. The research evidence may indicate that small is not only beautiful but also effective and efficient; yet day-to-day practice proceeds on the basic assumption that big is better, however discredited this assumption may be. Catholic social theory should be arguing that the only way the trend can be reversed is if experiments such as new approaches to automobile construction (pioneered by Volvo) are proved to be at least as efficient and probably more efficient than giantism. For all practical purposes, since giantism currently is in complete possession of the economy and the society, those who believe in decentralization and smallness and subsidiarity are going to have to

---

were actually born in the city. Queens and Staten Island have far more in common with the north side of Chicago than either does with Midtown or the Lake Shore limousine districts of Chicago.

prove that their way is not only efficient but more efficient; they are going to have to carry the day by beating the centralizers at their own game, by establishing that greater productivity and more money can be made by treating individuals as persons and not as cogs in a machine. The Catholic social theorist believes in principle that that is so. It is time for him to acquire the technical skill that he needs to demonstrate how his principles might be effectively applied in practice. Indeed, the greatest single obstacle at the present time to a serious consideration of a Catholic social theory as an alternative to capitalism or socialism is that the Church simply does not have available the technical or the professional competence to demonstrate how its implicit, often unselfconscious view of human nature and society can be applied in practice to the world as we now know it. Perhaps the reason why Catholic social spokesmen settle for romanticism or utopia or anger at the United States is the realization that they are simply incapable of saying how someone might apply the Catholic world view to the practical realities of every day economic and social living. Utopias come much easier than getting the kind of training and experience you need to know what you're talking about.

I'm neither an economist nor a specialist in the sociological study of large organizations. I realize as I set out the tentative propositions in this segment of the paper how naïve they are and how many legal, administrative, financial, and social difficulties stand in the way of even the modest social reforms implicit in the questions I raise. Again, Catholicism is paying the price for not having trained enough experts in new fields of knowledge in the past twenty years, and for abandoning concern for its valuable heritage of ideas ten years ago. We have a theory of human society that suddenly looks very attractive (though it does not appear explicitly Catholic) to many of our fellow citizens. We dimly remember, as I did in the office on Massachusetts Avenue, that these were the things we heard and even said long ago, but we simply do not have the knowledge or the skill or the experience to be able to suggest various ways that the society could be restructured in the light of our own theory. That is what Chesterton would have called a paradox, and the honest among us would admit it is a terrible embarrassment.

I hope it has become clear that the Catholic social theory of which I speak is not derived merely from abstract principles. Like any good theory, it is the product of both induction and deduction, of reflection on experience, the reinterpretation of that reflection in general propositions, and then the application once again of those propositions for testing and verification in the practical order. In the past, too much emphasis was placed on the deduction of a Catholic plan for restructuring society from St. Thomas, the papal encyclicals, or a frequently romanticized version of what life was like in the Middle Ages. In this book I have tried to rely more on analysis of and a reflection about the Catholic grassroots, unselfconscious experience of a social theory and the various social-science research findings that seem to underpin and validate the Catholic theoretical perspective.

CHAPTER 8

❦ ❦ ❦

The Decline of Modernity, or Daniel Bell Is Wrong

A USEFUL exercise in trying to expound a point of view is to contrast it with another point of view with which one shares many fundamental agreements. To illustrate, therefore, what seems to me to be a Catholic social-theoretical perspective on the present situation in American society, I propose to contrast the viewpoint on which this book is based with that which has been brilliantly expressed recently by Daniel Bell in his book *The Cultural Contradictions of Capitalism*.[1] Bell is an intriguing mixture of old Trotskyist and new Tory. Many of his criticisms of contemporary culture in society I find most attractive, but nevertheless I have some fundamental and basic disagreements with him. If one approaches society from the viewpoint shaped by Catholic assumptions, one will be profoundly skeptical not so much about Bell's criticisms of society as about the assumptions that seem implicit in his description of what he criticizes. Bell may very well be right about the present state of American society, but someone looking at the social order from the Catholic perspective would demand very powerful evidence to back up his analysis, because the Catholic predisposition would have grave reservations about whether the organic society could possibly deteriorate as far as Bell seems to think it has.

Let me first sketch out areas of agreement.

1. First, I accept Bell's description of the triumph of modernity in the high culture:

In the culture, we have the rise of the independent artist, released from church and princely patron, writing and painting what pleases him rather than his sponsor; the market will make him free. In the development of culture, this search for independence, the will to be free not only of patron but of all conventions, finds its expression in modernism and, in its extreme form, in the idea of the untrammeled self.

2. I agree with Bell (and Trilling, who coined the phrase) that modernity has in effect become an "adversary culture." Bell quotes Irving Howe, who is quite correct when he says, "modernity consists in revolt against the prevalent style, *an unyielding rage against the official order.*" Bell states that "The legend of modernism is that of the free creative spirit at war with the bourgeoisie." He adds:

> Who in the world today, especially in the world of culture, defends the bourgeoisie? Yet in the domain of those who think themselves serious about culture, and of their widespread and trailing *epigoni*, the legend of the free creative spirit now at war, no longer merely with bourgeois society but with "civilization" or "repressive tolerance" or some other agency that curtails "freedom," still sustains an adversary culture.

Bell is certainly right when he quotes Trilling as saying that any historian of literature of the modern age will take for granted that modern writing is subversive, that it intends to detach the reader from the habits of thought and feeling that the larger culture imposes.

3. I agree with Bell that the adversary culture dominates the cultural order and that its members "substantially influence, if not dominate, the cultural establishments today: the publishing houses, museums, and galleries; the major news, picture, and cultural weeklies and monthlies; the theater, the cinema, and the universities." They may, incidentally, be in revolt against the bourgeoisie, but they tend to lead very bourgeois lives themselves—complete with the summer homes in Cape Cod or Martha's Vineyard, a point Bell seems to miss. If the adversary culture is in endless revolt against the establishment, it is, it seems to me, also an endless phony revolt. However, Bell is

certainly correct in describing how impresarios of the cultural establishment think of themselves:

> Today, each new generation, starting off at the benchmarks attained by the adversary culture of its cultural parents, declares in sweeping fashion that the status quo represents backward conservatism or repression, so that, in a widening gyre, new and fresh assaults on the social structure are mounted.

4. I also agree with Bell that modernity is in a serious state of decline:

> Today modernism is exhausted. There is no tension. The creative impulses have gone slack. It has become an empty vessel. The impulse to rebellion has been institutionalized by the "cultural mass" and its experimental forms have become the syntax and semiotics of advertising and haute couture. As a cultural style, it exists as radical chic, which allows the cultural mass the luxury of "freer" life-styles while holding comfortable jobs within an economic system that has itself been transformed in its motivations.

In a footnote to this passage, Bell quotes Octavio Paz, the modernist poet, as saying, "Today . . . we are living the end of the *idea of modern art.*" Bell notes, "My only quarrel would be with the word 'today.' I believe that modernism lost its power 50 years ago." To anticipate my disagreement with Bell, I would wonder how much power it has ever had on ordinary people.

5. I agree with Bell's "unfashionable answer" as to what the future holds, that is, "The return of Western society to some conception of religion."

But my disagreements with Bell are also systematic.

1. First, as the reader doubtless knows by now, I do not accept the modernization model as an adequate description of the social change of the last several centuries. Bell nevertheless seems to; indeed, he accepts it in its classic and unreformed fashion:

The fundamental assumption of modernity, the thread that has run through Western civilization since the sixteenth century, is that the social unit of society is not the group, the guild, the tribe, or the city, but the person. The Western ideal was the autonomous man who, in becoming self-determining, would achieve freedom. With this "new man" there was a repudiation of institutions (the striking result of the Reformation, which installed individual conscience as the source of judgment); the opening of new geographical and social frontiers; the desire, and the growing ability, to master nature and to make of oneself what one can, and even, in discarding old roots, to remake oneself altogether. What began to count was not the past but the future.

Now from my perspective as both a collector of survey data and a neighborhood-rooted parish priest, I immediately want to say to Bell's "What began to count was not the past but the future," the future for whom? And for how many? And to what extent? I just don't know how future-obsessed most folks are. I do not know how many of them really take autonomous man as an ideal, and how many really want to remake themselves altogether. It is, I think, a researchable question. Most of the ordinary people I know either have strong roots or desperately want them. In the world of Columbia, Harvard, and corporate Midtown Manhattan what Bell is describing may have happened to some people, but I am profoundly skeptical about it—at least that it happened so simply and so without qualification in the neighborhoods and the towns of America.

2. Nor am I as ready to believe as Bell is that the Protestant ethic and the Puritan temper have vanished in American society.

Changes in culture as a whole, particularly the emergence of new life-styles, are made possible not only by changes in sensibility, but also by shifts in the social structure itself. One can see this most readily, in American society, in the development of new buying habits in a high consumption economy and the resultant erosion of the Protestant ethic and the Puritan temper, the two codes which sustained the traditional value system of American bourgeois society. It is the breakup of this ethic and temper, owing as much to changes in social structure as to changes in the culture, that has undercut the beliefs and legitimations that sanctioned work and reward in American society. It is this transformation and the lack of any rooted new ethic that are responsible, in good part, for the sense of disorientation and dismay that marks the public mood today.

Again I want to know who, how many, and to what extent these "two codes which sustained the traditional value system of American bourgeois society" have vanished. The Protestant ethic, with all its emphasis on hard work and achievement, is certainly alive and well among the eastern and southern European ethnic groups in the large cities. And I can testify, through my years of parish ministry to the affluent Irish, that achievement, success, hard work, industry, and sexual repression have not vanished from the American earth. Even the "adversary culture" types seem to work terribly hard and seem quite incapable of relaxing when they do depart for the Vineyard and other watering spots. And much of the ecological environmental insistence on frugality is profoundly Puritan in spirit. Nor can Bell successfully compare the sexual permissiveness of our day with that of Puritan times because all we know about the early history of the colonies indicates that the Puritans were not in fact all that sexually repressive—despite their name.

3. I also reject the sophisticated blending of the "mass society" and "future shock" models that is Bell's description of contemporary America.

"The automobile, the motion picture, and radio are technological in origin: advertising, planned obsolescence, and credit are all socological innovations." Doubtless such innovations have made things different than they were in the past, but I do not believe that the increase in "number, interaction, self-confidences, and time orientation" has in fact produced "mass society" or "future-oriented society" or a "sensate society."

What is distinctive, then, about contemporary society is not only its size and number, but the increased interaction—both physical (through travel, larger work units, and greater housing densities) and psychic (through the mass media)—which ties us to so many other persons, directly and symbolically. Increased interaction leads not only to social differentiations but, as a mode of experience, to psychic differentiation as well—to the desire for change and novelty, to the search for sensation, and to the syncretism of culture, all of which mark so distinctively the rhythm of contemporary life.

Reality breaks down when the confirming "others" have lost their meaning for the person seeking to locate himself or find a place in the society. The sociological problem of reality in our time—in terms of social location and identity—arises because individuals have left old anchorages, no longer follow inherited ways, are constantly faced with the problems of choice (the ability to choose careers, life-styles, friends, or political representatives is, for the mass of people, something new in social history), and no longer find authoritative standards or critics to guide them. The change from family and class to generation as the "structural" source of confirmation thus creates new strains in identity.

I simply don't know many people who spend very much of their time seeking for novelty or new sensation. Bell is, I think, victim of the same fallacy Alvin Toffler is (though Toffler falls victim to it in a more simpleminded way). He describes the technological changes, particularly those in transportation and communication, vividly and dramatically and then says, "Obviously, such changes have had a profound impact on human sensibility." But this is precisely to beg the question: Why "obviously"? Maybe they have, maybe they haven't. Still, what we know about human nature, both from empirical research and from solidly grounded psychological theory, impresses us not so much with change as with continuity. Are we really all that different in our sensibility than our predecessors? Or do we merely know a little more, talk a little more, and move about a little more freely? I would submit that the answer to that question is a matter for research rather than for gratuitous assumption.

Nor am I persuaded that for a large number of people the "confirming others" have lost their meaning, or that social location and identity have been lost, or that many individuals have left old anchorages. Again, it is a matter for research and not for assumptions based on the obvious truth of a model that is itself an assumption. Bell is undoubtedly right that contemporary humans have a far wider range of choices than their predecessors, and this wider range of choices makes questions of values much more explicit than in the past. But it does not follow that one really can very effectively leap behind the fundamental values that one absorbed in the early socialization process. Doubtless a fair number of the members of the adversary culture have tried to do so, but they spend most of their lives—it seems to an outsider—fighting what they thought they had left behind.

Furthermore, I think that Bell too readily accepts the conventional wisdom about the generation gap. Most of the empirical evidence with which I am familiar suggests that, while the young people fight with their parents sometimes, most of them end up holding value patterns pretty much like those of their parents, though they may express them in slightly different fashion. I simply do not believe there is evidence that generation has replaced family or class as a source of confirmation—save for a very brief period of years (late teens and early twenties) and then probably for only a relatively small number of people. Some of the generation that matured during the 1960s may well have chosen the style of the youth culture for the rest of their lives. There are some Ph.D. candidates who are earning their upkeep as gardeners or cooks and living on vegetarian or macrobiotic diets, but they are only a tiny segment of the society. Bell, it seems to me, too easily takes as proven that which remains to be proved and assumes as universal that which, if it exists at all, is probably true for only a relative minority of the society. Bell would respond perhaps by arguing that it is an influential minority. That brings me to my fourth disagreement.

4. I do not think that the cultural elites are all that influential. In one of his more brilliantly written paragraphs, Bell seems to me to tip his hand.

> Fun morality centers, in most instances, on sex. And here the seduction of the consumer has become almost total. The most tell-tale illustration, I believe, was a double-page advertisement

by Eastern Airlines in the *New York Times*, in 1973, saying: "Take the Bob and Carol, Ted and Alice, Phil and Anne Vacation." The blatant theme was a takeoff on *Bob and Carol and Ted and Alice*, a sniggering film about the fumbling attempts of two friendly couples to engage in wife-swapping. Here was Eastern Airlines saying, in effect: "We will fly you down to the Caribbean. We will rent you a cabana. Fly now, pay later." Eastern does not tell you *what* you pay, but you can postpone the money (and forget the guilt) and take the Bob and Carol, Ted and Alice, and (for further titillation another couple is added) Phil and Anne vacation. Compare this with Franklin's 13 useful virtues, which included temperance, frugality, tranquillity, and chastity. At the turn of the century, a church in the Midwest might have property on which a brothel was located. And one could then at least say: "Well, we are losing bodies, but we are earning money to save souls." Today, when one sells bodies, one is no longer also saving souls.

Now after reading a paragraph like that—admittedly very clever—I feel like heaving the book against the opposite wall and shouting, "You really can't believe that!" Ben Franklin, to begin with, however much he talked about chastity, was not a model of it in practice, if I remember my history. And how many pretty people, even *New York Times* readers, are boarding Eastern Airlines to fly down to a Caribbean cabana to engage in wife-swapping? If anyone is being seduced by that kind of ad, it's Eastern Airlines, which has been deceived by its advertising agency into thinking that there are lots of people sitting around trying to find out a way to swap wives whose problems are solved when they pick up their *Times* and read the Eastern Airlines ad. Don't we really require a lot more evidence before we can be persuaded that such advertising has any effect at all—other than on the advertising budgets of the airlines and the incomes of their advertising agencies? Who is kidding whom? I am not sure, but I doubt very much that very many people in the neighborhoods of the country—even the affluent ones—are being kidded.

Underlying my disagreements with Daniel Bell, I think, are three principal differences. First of all, I simply do not believe that you can analyze a society solely by looking either at its high culture or at its mass media (especially when the mass media are to an ever increasing extent influenced by the modernity or the adversary assumptions of the high culture). Bell, it seems to me, has fallen victim to what I call the "Columbia lunchroom" fallacy. That is to say, the eager lunch conversations back in the 1930s and 1940s at Columbia about culture, art, philosophy, and politics may have been perfectly valid discussions of the environment around that university, but they are not valid means for analyzing a society as large, complex, diversified, and variegated as the American one. You need to bring in data from other sources—national surveys, participant observation, field work, or that obtained simply by living in a neighborhood.

Second, I simply cannot accept Bell's easy assumption that the cultural elites have all that much influence on the masses. On the contrary, the public I know seems to be systematically skillful at disbelieving everything it reads in the newspapers, sees on television, or is told by advertising agencies. The country is sufficiently large and variegated that there are enough consumers to keep the producers of elite culture and even upper-middle-belt culture gainfully employed (enabling them to pay the taxes and repair bills on their Vineyard homes). But do artists such as de Kooning and novelists such as Pynchon and musicians such as the Polish moderns have much influence on ordinary people (who are, let's say, 90 percent of the population)? This is something I profoundly doubt. To put the matter less strongly, it is something that is researchable and subject to proof but is not, I think, to be casually assumed.

Such novelists of modernity as Pynchon, Gardner, and Vonnegut, for example, can lead comfortable lives because there are some people in our society who enjoy their books, others who think they should read them, and still others who feel constrained to write dissertations about them; and yet most Americans do not in fact pay very much attention to such novels. If the elite novelists turn precious and academic in their modernity, then the typical American will have recourse to the storytellers, such as the various Donalds—Ross Macdonald, John MacDonald, and Donald Hamilton. Storytellers remain popular because the novelists of modernity have stopped being what novelists are supposed to be according to the ordinary folk—storytellers. Ordinary people, like their ancestors, still search for story and not for the anarchy of modernity.

I could make many similar arguments, but the point is clear: what remains to be investigated is the impact of the cultural elites on the rest of the country. The shape and dimensions of that impact are, it seems to me, no more self-evident prior to systematic research than is the impact of "future shock" or the existence of "mass society."

3. The most fundamental difference between Bell and me is that he assumes mass modernity is not only possible but that it has happened; and I assume that it is very unlikely to have happened. He assumes that the dense, informal, intimate network that supported human beings and their values in times past not only could be but in fact has been broken up. If I am skeptical about that, probably the reason is that my basic view of the fundamental social nature of humankind leads me to doubt that it can be broken up—at least for very long and for many people. The differences between me and Bell as to questions of fact are researchable, and once the facts are established the differences in theory and description about what *has* changed are at least arguable. But I wonder if we could either research or argue about fundamental positions on the social nature of human nature. Do we not then get into questions about the nature of the cosmos, the meaning of human life, and the identity of whatever basic force or forces are at work in the universe that go beyond research, discussion, speculation, and come very close to being matters of faith?

The point of this discussion is not to refute Daniel Bell, who is both a colleague and a friend, but to point out that someone who comes out of the Catholic tradition finds himself tending to look at social reality in a very different way than someone like Bell will look at it—though, of course, he will agree with many of the things Bell has said. Like Bell, a Catholic will be very skeptical about plans that purport to remake human nature quickly and reform human society soon. The Catholic, like the capitalist, the classic conservative (which Bell is), and the Manichaeans will be on the minus side of the remakability of human nature, though perhaps higher on that vector than the others (see Table IV); but the difference between the Catholics, on the one hand, and the conservatives, the capitalists, and the Manichaeans, on the other, will be on the modernization vector, which is in fact a "nature of human society" vector. In the previous chapter I suggested that the classic conservative position is that human nature is weakly social—so weak that the modernity that Bell criticizes is not merely a distinct possibility for a small elite of the society but a probability for the whole of society. More than that, Bell contends, it is something that has in fact actually happened. Someone under the influence of the Catholic organic view of society will almost certainly disagree. Most people most of the time, Catholics will suggest, are not alienated, cut off, isolated, autonomous individuals. Human nature is not weakly social, it is strongly, powerfully, inevitably social. Indeed to lift a line from Clifford Geertz, it was social even before it was human. Something has happened all right, but for most of us modernity isn't it.

So with all due respect and all proper nuance and qualification, a Catholic ends the discussion with "Daniel Bell is wrong."

Conclusion

As I have thought about the position taken in this book I have wondered whether I am reflecting on the high tradition of Catholic social theory as contained in the encyclicals and in the works of writers such as Maritain, Belloc, and Mounier or whether I am reflecting on my own personal experience and articulating a world view that I had before coming into contact with the high tradition. I rather incline to the thought that, like the Catholic labor leaders of the 1930s and 1940s (John Brophy, Philip Murray), I resonate positively to the social encyclicals because they articulate what I already feel in my bones to be true.

But my own experience is less important than that of the politicians, union leaders, parish priests, and immigration-era bishops who responded to their practical problems in an American urban environment out of hunch, instinct, and feel, with precious little need to refer to Leo XIII or Maritain—indeed, without being aware of the writings of either. The high tradition is, in other words, a formalization and an articulation of the insights and presuppositions of the low tradition.

David Tracy has suggested that the fundamental difference in theological style between the two Christian traditions is that the Protestant style is dialectical and the Catholic style is analogic. One can readily apply this insight to the two social theories of Catholicism and Protestantism. The Catholic theory uses the analogue of the human body and sees the person integrated into an organic society, whereas the Protestant theory—from which I suggest both capitalism and socialism are heresies—sees the person and society in dialectical opposition to one another. Whether the theological style or the perceptual style are prior would make an interesting debating point, though as a social scientist I would be inclined to give the nod to the latter.

If there are different views of reality or different ways of viewing reality that separate the two Christian traditions, one must begin to ask about the dynamics of the transmission of these differences in the intimacy of the family and peer-group environment, perhaps long before the child ever hears about religion. Very little research has been done on this subject, though my colleagues William and Nancy McCready have argued that fundamental world view and sexual self-definition are acquired at the same time and indeed in the same experience.* Their argument is persuasive but hardly conclusive until much more evidence has been gathered.

If the reader wonders whether the Catholic social theory is reactionary or radical, left or right, conservative or liberal, then I have failed in my task, because I have tried to argue throughout this book that such questions can be asked only if one makes the very rigid assumption that the available alternatives for organizing human life in the modern world are capitalism or socialism. If one cannot see beyond that perspective, then Catholic social theory is obviously irrelevant. It is, however, surely reactionary in the sense that it rejects the idea that evolutionary progress has eliminated the primordial and the

---

* William C. and Nancy G. McCready, "The Origins of Religious Persistence: Sexual Identity and Religious Socialization," *Concilium*, Vol. 1, No. 9, 1973. William McCready is preparing a book on "fathering" based on his finding that in white American society, at any rate, religious socialization seems to be primarily a paternal process. However, to even things out, he finds the mother to be the more effective political socializing agent—and also to have more religious influence on the father than he has on her.

particularistic from the human condition; it is also reactionary in that it suggests that heterogeneity, particularism, primordial ties, and primary group relationships are not to be ignored by social planners, policy-makers, and administrators. Yet it is profoundly radical in that it rejects the basic and fundamental assumptions on which both capitalism and socialism are based, as well as the perspective within which the capitalism-versus-socialism debate occurs. It says to Marx and Adam Smith, "You are both wrong; and what's more, you are both Protestants."

It is also conservative in the sense that it believes in conserving such fundamental institutions as neighborhood, family, village, community; but it is liberal, indeed radically liberal, in its demand that human beings be freed from the oppressive chains of the large corporate bureaucracy (and it doesn't give a hoot which ideology underpins the bureaucracy).

Catholic social theory is not seeking to reconstruct the past. This particular theorist has no desire to return to County Mayo; Cook County suits him just fine, but he does believe that in the past there was a wisdom built up through the ages that the present and the future can ill afford to ignore. Chicago and New York have something to learn from County Mayo and also something to learn from places like Beverly, Astoria, or Forest Hills. There is no reason why the modern world should learn these things, however, if the Catholic Church, which has experienced both County Mayo and Beverly, refuses to speak of its own experience or to speculate about what that experience might provide for the building of a better world. Let this book stand as a restatement of an alternative to capitalism, socialism, and anarchism—an alternative shared by many traditions and one to which Catholicism was, at least until recently, deeply committed.

Notes

Chapter 1

1. E. F. Schumacher, *Small Is Beautiful*. New York: Harper & Row, 1973; paperback edition, Perennial Library, 1975.
2. David Matza, *Delinquency and Drift*. New York: Wiley, 1964, p. 3.
3. Ian Barbour, *Myths, Models, and Paradigms: A Comparative Study in Science and Religion*. New York: Harper & Row, 1974.
4. See, for example, William C. McCready, "The Origins of Religious Persistence: Sexual Identity and Religious Socialization," *Concilium: An International Review of Theology*, 9 (1973), pp. 58–68.
5. Charles Shanabruch, *The Chicago Catholic Church's Role as an Americanizer, 1893–1928*, Ph.D. dissertation, University of Chicago, 1975.

Chapter 2

1. Clifford Geertz, "Ideology as a Cultural System," in *The Interpretation of Cultures: Selected Essays by Clifford Geertz*. New York: Basic Books, 1973, pp. 193–233.

Chapter 3

1. Nick Eberstadt, "Myths of the Food Crisis," *New York Review of Books*, February 19, 1976, pp. 32–37.
2. *Ibid.*, p. 37.
3. Christopher Lasch, "The Family and History," *New York Review of Books*, v. 22, no. 18, 13th Nov., pp. 33–38, 1975; "The Emotions of Family Life," v. 22, no. 19, 27th Nov., pp. 37–42, 1975; "What the Doctor Ordered," v. 22, no. 20, 11th Dec., pp. 50–54, 1975.
4. Edward Shorter, *The Making of the Modern Family*. New York: Basic Books, 1975.
5. Michael Gordon, ed., *The American Family in Social-Historical Perspective*. New York: St. Martin's Press, 1973.
6. Robert Nisbet, *The Sociological Tradition*. New York: Basic Books, 1966.
7. Peter Laslett, with the assistance of Richard Wall, ed., *Household and Family in Past Time*. Cambridge, England: The Cambridge University Press, 1972.
8. Jack Goody, "The Evolution of the Family," in Laslett, ed., *Household and Family in Past Time*, p. 124.
9. Lasch, *op. cit.*, "What the Doctor Ordered," p. 53.
10. Thomas Luckmann, *The Invisible Religion*. New York: Macmillan, 1967.
11. Lynn White, Jr., "The Historical Roots of Our Ecologic Crisis," *Science*, 155 (March 10, 1967), 1203.
12. Donella Meadows *et al.*, *The Limits to Growth*. New York: Universe Books, 1972; reprinted by New American Library, 1972.

Chapter 4

1. Noam Chomsky, *Reflections on Language*. New York: Pantheon Books, 1976, p. 126.
2. *Ibid.*, p. 133.
3. *Ibid.*
4. *Ibid.*, pp. 133–134.
5. *Ibid.*, p. 134.

6. Loren Eiseley, *The Firmament of Time*. New York: Atheneum Publishers, 1962.

7. William C. Pollard, "The Uniqueness of the Earth," in Ian G. Barbour, ed. *Earth Might Be Fair*. Englewood Cliffs, N.J.: Prentice-Hall, 1972, p. 94.

8. *Ibid.*, pp. 95–96.

9. Loren Eiseley, "Man, the Lethal Factor," *American Scientist* (March 1963), pp. 78ff.

10. Daniel Bell, *The Cultural Contradictions of Capitalism*. New York: Basic Books, 1976, p. 5.

11. Reinhold Niebuhr, *The Nature and Destiny of Man*, 2 vols. *Vol. I: Human Nature*. New York: Charles Scribner's Sons, 1964, pp. 178–179.

12. *Ibid.*, p. 182.

13. *Ibid.*, p. 185.

14. Donald T. Campbell, "On the Conflicts Between Biological and Social Evolution and Between Psychology and Moral Tradition," *American Psychologist*, 30 (December 1975), 1103–1126.

15. *Ibid.*, pp. 1116–1117.

16. See Henri Rondet, *Original Sin, the Patristic and Theological Background*. Shannon, Ireland: Ecclesia Press, 1972.

17. Niebuhr, *op. cit.*, pp. 247–248.

Chapter 5

1. E. F. Schumacher, *Small Is Beautiful*. New York: Harper & Row, 1973, p. 181.

2. *Ibid.*, p. 165.

3. *Ibid.*

4. Emmanuel Mounier, *Personalism*. London: Routledge & Kegan Paul, 1952, pp. 18–19.

5. Peter Berger, *Pyramids of Sacrifice: Political Ethics and Social Change*. New York: Basic Books, 1975.

6. Jacques Maritain, *True Humanism*. London: Geoffrey Bles, The Centenary Press, 1938, p. 19.

7. George Woodcock, *Anarchism: A History of Libertarian Ideas and Movements*. New York: World Publications/Meridian Books, 1962.

8. *Ibid.*, p. 476.
9. *Ibid.*, p. 25.
10. *Ibid.*
11. *Ibid.*, p. 26.
12. *Ibid.*, p. 27.
13. *Ibid.*
14. *Ibid.*, p. 33.
15. *Ibid.*, p. 34.

Chapter 6

1. F. J. Roethlisberger and William J. Dickson, *Management and the Worker*. Cambridge, Mass.: Harvard University Press, 1939.
2. Philip Slater, *Earthwalk*. Garden City, N.Y.: Doubleday, 1974.
3. Manning Nash, *Machine Age Maya*. Chicago: University of Chicago Press, 1958, p. 144.
4. *Ibid.*
5. Lloyd Rudolph and Suzanne Rudolph, *The Modernity of Tradition*. Chicago: University of Chicago Press, 1967, p. 3.
6. Clifford Geertz, *The Religion of Java*. New York: The Free Press of Glencoe, 1960.
7. Alex Inkeles and David H. Smith, *Becoming Modern*. Cambridge, Massachusetts: Harvard University Press, 1974.
8. Edward Laumann, *Bonds of Pluralism: The Form and Substance of Urban Social Networks*. New York: Wiley Interscience, 1973.
9. James Q. Wilson and Edward C. Banfield, "Political Ethos Revisited," *American Political Science Review*, 65 (December 1971), 1048–62.
10. Terry N. Clark, "The Irish Ethic and the Spirit of Patronage," *Ethnicity* 2 (December 1975), 305–359.
11. *Ibid.*, p. 321.
12. *Ibid.*, p. 322.
13. Sidney Verba and Norman H. Nie, *Participation in America: Political Democracy and Social Equality*. New York: Harper & Row, 1972.

14. The data were collected in a study of women's political activism in Chicago, in which both activist and non-activist women were interviewed.

Chapter 8

1. All references in this chapter are to Daniel Bell's *The Cultural Contradictions of Capitalism*. New York: Basic Books, 1976.

Index

About the Author

Andrew M. Greeley, a leading Catholic thinker, is currently Director of the Center for the Study of American Pluralism at the National Opinion Research Center in Chicago. He received his Ph.D. from the University of Chicago and is also a Roman Catholic priest. Father Greeley has lectured widely and has an international reputation. He is the author of over twenty books in the fields of sociology and religion.